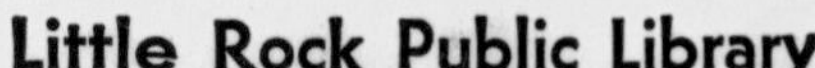

THE COMPANY SHE KEPT

Books by Doris Grumbach

Nonfiction

THE COMPANY SHE KEPT

Fiction

THE SHORT THROAT, THE TENDER MOUTH

THE SPOIL OF THE FLOWERS

DORIS GRUMBACH

The Company She Kept

Coward-McCann, Inc.
New York

Library of Congress Catalog Card Number: 66-26531

PRINTED IN THE UNITED STATES OF AMERICA

For Barbara Helen Remers, one of
the best of the company I've *kept.*

For permission to reprint copyrighted material, the author wishes to thank the following:

Alfred A. Knopf, Inc. for *Pictures from an Institution* by Randall Jarrell, published by Meridian Books, 1960; Brandt & Brandt for *The Company She Keeps,* by Mary McCarthy, published by Harcourt, Brace and World, Inc., copyright ©, 1939, 1941, 1942 by Mary McCarthy, copyright renewed, 1967, by Mary McCarthy, and for *The Oasis,* by Mary McCarthy, published by New American Library, copyright ©, 1949 by Mary McCarthy; Esquire, Inc. for "Mary McCarthyism," by Brock Brower, published July, 1962; Farrar, Straus & Giroux, Inc. for *On the Contrary,* by Mary McCarthy, published by Farrar, Straus and Cudahy, 1961, copyright ©, 1953-61 by Mary McCarthy and "The Vassar Girl," by Mary McCarthy, copyright ©, 1951 by Curtiss Publishing Company, reprinted by permission of Farrar, Straus & Giroux, Inc.; *The New Yorker* for "The Company Is Not Responsible," by Mary McCarthy, published April 22, 1944; Harcourt, Brace & World, Inc., for *Cast a Cold Eye* by Mary McCarthy, published 1950, *A Charmed Life,* by Mary McCarthy, published 1955, *The Groves of Academe,* by Mary McCarthy, published 1951, *The Group,* by Mary McCarthy, published 1963, and *Memories of a Catholic Girlhood,* by Mary McCarthy, published 1957; *The Paris Review* for excerpts from an interview with Mary McCarthy, published in issue no. 27, Winter, 1961 and by The Viking Press, Inc., in their *Writers at Work* series.

Contents

Author's Note

I AM grateful to Mary McCarthy for the time she spent with me, the material and pictures she made available, and for her tolerance of my often impertinent questions.

I acknowledge also the use of an excellent bibliography of Mary McCarthy's work by Sherli Goldman of Los Angeles, to be published by Harcourt, Brace & World, Inc.

Foreword

IN a review of *Pale Fire* that Mary McCarthy published in *Encounter* some years ago, she speaks of "the occupational mania of commentators." The hero of that novel, the mad Kimbote, who is annotating a dead poet's work, "has convinced himself that the poem is in a sense *his* poem . . . and cannot properly be understood without his gloss." I am in Kimbote's position, feeling as I do a certain sense of possession of my subject—as if, foolishly, *she* were *mine*. This occupational mania may account for my posturing in this book as an authority on What She Means or What She Meant to be Understood by You, and as the owner of all the answers about a subject who is very much alive and might well answer them far better or differently than I. I apologize for my proprietary attitude, developed after a year of reading Mary McCarthy, her critics, and the works she has declared in print she admires, but I shall hold to it nonetheless, on the theory that what can be said about a writer like Mary McCarthy might possibly cast some light on a whole generation of novelists, feminine and not, and critics of them, while at the same time it occasionally illuminates its subject.

Let me confess right out, and at the start, another symptom

of my monomania, a certain impatience with much that has been written about Mary McCarthy by critics, reviewers, and interviewers. Even in the few cases where a critic manages to say some acute things about her or her work he customarily (as if by some compulsion of *his* own) will embed them in near nonsense, misquotation, or what seems to me to be misunderstanding of her intent or her accomplishment. (Of course I am aware that I am in grave danger of having this accusation brought home to me by virtue of having myself ventured into the arena of judgment, but that, after all, is what makes the critic's life interesting and profitable.) This is true of such "major" misinterpreters as Norman Podhoretz, Norman Mailer, Dean Robert E. Fitch, John Aldridge and even, to a far lesser degree, Louis Auchincloss. It is far more true of minor writers like Bruce Cook, who touches some truths while at the same time paralleling them with misreadings: he cannot, for example, understand why Mary McCarthy was "as harsh as she was on the Prestons," in *Memories of a Catholic Girlhood,* although in truth her portrait of her Jewish grandmother is one of the most sympathetic and compassionate she has written; he describes Martha Sinnott in *A Charmed Life* as "sentenced" to death for her misdemeanor (adultery with her ex-husband), but nowhere in the novel is there any indication of a causal relationship between the two events. Norman Podhoretz, on the other hand, misreads the irony of the last paragraph of that novel by thinking that "at that moment her car swerves and crashes, killing her instantly," although what actually happens is that she is crashed *into* as she hugs her side of the road. A small point, but important to the reading of Martha's death which happens as she conforms to one law on her way to defying another.

These extensions of the facts of a writer's work into the

fiction of misinterpretation are more common in what is written about Mary McCarthy than in criticism about many other modern writers, and they seem to proliferate in direct proportion to the relatively modest body of fiction she has produced. It is remarkable that such a small amount of good prose has produced so much bad criticism, that in the course of such a relatively short life there have been so many well-meaning excursions into error. There are of course a few kindly critics like John Chamberlain and Elizabeth Hardwick, but their work on Mary McCarthy seems to damn her by its very mildness and indecisiveness, like indulgent parents with an unruly child.

Further, it is easy in Mary McCarthy's case to find entirely contradictory statements made in good faith by serious critics, statements which result in two separate systems of thought concerning her work, each well-reasoned and each, it seems to me, equally wrong-headed. The arguments rage as to whether she is a moralist or not, whether she is honest, morally naïve, or downright dishonest, whether she is candid and aboveboard or sly and vindictive, whether her lost faith or her libertarian optimism has influenced her more. She is attacked from the far right and the far left with equal force. It is amusing to note that a recent piece of hers, a report on a student meeting in Paris, was printed in *Encounter* after having been rejected first by a left-wing publication and then by one on the right. (It did however find a French home in *Preuves.*) One man will interpret a character like Martha Sinnott as a victim of her own unfeminine insistence upon the truth. She becomes, in another system of criticism, "an ugly character with a fair façade." To one, Mary McCarthy's "intention is satiric"; to another her intention is vicious and personally spiteful. She is at the core "compassionate." No, not at all, "she abhors humanity." She is "not at home in the theatre"; she is "certainly the best American writer to have written about the American theatre in our generation." She is "a cat whose novels produce ailurophobia in male critics," "she has a basilisk eye," she is a "heartless chronicler," she has "malicious accuracy of detail," "she wants to put everything in," "she leaves too much out." Scornful, tender, clever, condescending, detached, cool, cold, ironic, vengeful, uncharitable, she has been said to be all of these. The only subject about which there is no argument whatever is the quality of her prose. And curiously, while the excellence of her style is conceded on all sides, it is rarely analyzed, although it would seem that such an analysis would reveal much that is relevant to her whole "case," just as she herself has insisted that better and more informed writing about the art and craft of acting would enhance the value of dramatic criticism.

Perhaps her worst enemies are the occasional voices of over-praise. They are, as it were, a Greek chorus of admiring critics who occupy the plot at every crucial turn and leave little for her to say directly to the reader. Elizabeth Hardwick's extravagant opinion of Mary McCarthy's essays, "The Fact in Fiction" and "Characters in Fiction," that the ideas expressed in them "are the only new things said about the art of the novel in many years," is surely as extravagant as *Time*'s "quite possibly the cleverest writer the U.S. has ever produced" (a view she herself detests because of her suspicion of the adjective "clever"), or the view of her unquestioned pre-eminence as critic of the theatre in our time for which Gore Vidal was responsible. Norman Mailer, in reviewing *The Group,* accused her of "the accumulated vanity of being over-praised through the years for too little and so being pleased with herself for too little"; "overpetted" she is, he says. There may of course be some grain of truth in this; a writer may often be, not the object of, but ultimately the victim of critical extravagance.

Perhaps the most damaging accusation is that, in contradiction to Louis Auchincloss's view that Mary McCarthy is related to Sarah Orne Jewett and Edith Wharton in her efforts to "preserve traditions in our own century," her real aim is to be not a caretaker of what is still of value in her era but a wrecker of it all. Her satirical powers are directed toward total destruction of what she has found hateful; she is not only interested in cleaning out the stables of the intellectuals, the bohemians, the educated and the academicians, but, in the process, burns them to the ground. Or, to change the image, she is a satirist of such fury that she throws the baby away with the dirty bathwater.

If what has been written is not to be wholly trusted, partly because it is contradictory and partly because it is either scurrilous or extravagant, the thing to do then is to try a fresh approach upon the target, scan the maps already drawn up and the evidence gathered and see if the writer comes through any more clearly than she does out of the welter of thirty years of confusing and contradictory criticism. Biography is the starting point, with all its pitfalls, for in the case of Mary McCarthy it cannot be avoided. It is here, as it must be apparent to any close reader, that she herself takes her impetus as a writer.

Because of my conviction that the fiction of Mary McCarthy is autobiographical to an extraordinary degree, in the widest sense of autobiography,* I have chosen to move rather freely from the *facts* of her life, as they are known to me from a number of sources, including her own writing, her

* Mary McCarthy's own view of this is more limited: "I wouldn't call those things so much autobiography that are not part of one's own life. I mean that I consider the story of a marriage is autobiography. . . ."

conversations with me and with others, and private correspondence, to her *fictional* accounts of persons, places and events, and then back again. I trust the reader will follow me in these perhaps eccentric procedures and realize that, as at a Chinese dinner, I am dipping into a variety of sauces in order to season my work. If I were dealing with a writer whose product was almost entirely imaginative this kind of treatment would not be useful, would not indeed yield enough evidence for a critical approach. In the case of Mary McCarthy there is only a faint line between what really happened to her, the people she knew and knows, including herself, and the characters in her fictions. So I have made, in the following account, one fabric of these diverse threads. Certainly, the reader will understand, however, that in no case am I suggesting that *all* elements in any fiction are autobiographical or that to identify the author with her heroine at any point in her fiction suggests a total identification at all points in the fiction.

I am well aware that since she is a writer of fiction, Mary McCarthy's memory of events may not be entirely reliable. In addition, in some places the reader will no doubt sense my reserve in regard to some facts, a reserve which is necessary in order not to invade the privacy of a living person. I have become aware, in the process of writing this book, that one is not entirely free to prove one's assertions about the fictional uses of autobiography, either because the subject resists the attempt or because to do so involves other persons, equally sensitive about their privacy.

Finally, it will be noticed that I have taken the titles of chapters from her titles of her books. She has said that the titles are usually the clue to her books; in this case I have changed their form somewhat to make them the clue to the material in the chapter.

I *Of a Catholic Girlhood*

"I don't believe in God. My belief is nobody believes in God any more except peasants and simple people; the others just pretend to."

—INTERVIEW, *Life*, 1963.

HOW much of value does biography tell us about a writer? The answer is a truism. In some cases, where the writer is wholly dependent on himself as subject matter, a great deal, and in others proportionately little. In the study of a novelist like Dickens or Henry Fielding biography can be an interesting thing in itself, but it is not indispensable to a reading of their novels. Too often, much space and energy devoted to biographical data in a work of literary criticism is evidence of the critic's overweening interest in gossip and hearsay, or of his inability or unwillingness to deal with the thinking of the writer; this kind of criticism sells well but says, often, very little of lasting interest about the works of the subject. Ours is an age of gossip. In our time the public is far more interested in the writer than the writer's products, and this has produced a new kind of writer, one who lives colorfully in order to write in the same tone, one who becomes his own subject and whose experiences are planned as subject matter: Ernest Hemingway is the principal of this school. Richard Altick, in *The Art of Literary Research,* claims that this desire, on the part of the public, to "know" about an author is understandable: "As human beings we have an uneradicable and perfectly valid desire to know what fellowman created the work of art we admire. . . . Seldom is an artistic work an isolated entity which can be explained and judged solely in terms of itself."

Biographical data has importance in Mary McCarthy's case only if we do not stop with it. Over a period of years she has provided much of the factual material herself, so one can claim no great "finds" as a result of "research." She is her own best researcher, her own most honest biographer. She has confessed in her early work (until, one presumes, *The Group,* and perhaps including it) that she was "interested in the quest for self," an interest she professes now to have lost since "I don't know any more today than I did in 1941 about what my identity is . . . I've stopped looking for it."

She describes her own background as "polychrome." Her mother's father was a western lawyer, Harold Preston, of Protestant New England ancestry. Her mother's mother, Augusta Morganstern (immortalized in one of her most celebrated portraits, "Ask Me No Questions," as "the most beautiful woman in Seattle" and called "Gussie"), was born in San Francisco of Jewish parents who had been forty-niners. "After '48, after the failure of the '48 revolutions in Europe, hope for an equalitarian Europe really died, and the 48'ers, many of them, went to California in the Gold Rush as 49'ers. My great-grandfather, from central Europe, was one of them." Central Europe was probably Posen. "The word Posen somehow rings a bell to me now," she says. Her father's parents, wealthy James H. McCarthy and Elizabeth Sheridan

McCarthy, were second-generation Irish farm-settlers who got rich in grain elevators in Duluth and Minneapolis. "Before that, the family had been farmers in North Dakota and, before that . . . in Nova Scotia," where they had come from Ireland for religious rather than economic reasons and where "they became 'wreckers,' a common species of land pirate . . . tying lanterns at night to their sheep on the rocky cliffs to simulate a beaconing port and lure ships to their destruction, for the sake of plunder, or . . . for the sake of the salvage contract. Plunder would be more romantic, and I hope that was it." Mary McCarthy was thus the child of an Irish-Catholic father and a part-Jewish mother. The Protestant strain is from her maternal grandfather, Harold Preston, about whose immortal soul she was to worry so in convent school.

The wild strain of land pirate McCarthy looks is noticeable in pictures of Mary McCarthy's father, a remarkably handsome man, with thick, pompadoured, prematurely grey hair ("my father was grey" at twenty), with "very fair skin and queer lit-up grey-green electric eyes, fringed by" long, black thick eyelashes. He has, in his photographs, the look of many romantic-looking men, a certain Byronic, brooding quality, a melancholy which, in handsome men, takes on an almost mystic quality, although she herself remembers that he had a very light-hearted look. His animal magnetism, or what his daughter has called "a certain mythic power," may account for the tales told about him by his brother, Harry. Hoped by Mary McCarthy to be apocryphal, the story revealed that this romantic-looking progeny of land pirates was a periodic drunkard, a passer of bad checks to support his wild bouts, a black sheep who was, as a last resort, sent out west where he met Tess Preston. Roy's daughter refuses to believe all this.

"Uncle Harry's derelict brother, Roy, is not the same person as my father. I simply do not recognize him."

The McCarthy women were "pious and plain." This is especially apparent in Elizabeth McCarthy who "looked like a bulldog" and was a dogged, dogmatic Catholic. Her sons all married good-looking Protestant wives "as if to be ornery." The combination of Roy Winfield McCarthy and Therese Preston that produced the four McCarthy children was both contrary and fortunate. In two of them at least the "wrecker" looks are almost intact, with none of Elizabeth McCarthy's caninity.

Roy and Tess met at a summer resort in Oregon during a summer vacation. Tess was still an undergraduate at the University of Washington, and Roy, who had been graduated from the University of Minnesota, was attending Washington University Law School. She "was a beautiful, popular girl with an attractive, husky singing voice," and he was extraordinarily good-looking. "Both my parents were handsome, winning and romantic." This account sounds like the customarily unrealistic, highly colored nostalgia of a girl whose last memories of her parents come from her sixth year; however, the pictures of her parents and their young children included in *Memories of a Catholic Girlhood* are evidence of the truth of her memories.

Both the McCarthys and the Prestons opposed the marriage; it took place nonetheless in 1911 "in the big house overlooking Lake Washington in Seattle." Religion raised some difficulty; more important was Roy's precarious health. Doctors had predicted that his bad heart might give out at any moment: Mary McCarthy says that at the time of his marriage he was "an invalid." The Preston prophecy was that Roy would die young and leave his wife with a pack of children. Only the newlyweds, it seems, were apparently carefree.

The wedding was small "with chiefly family present." Tess McCarthy became a Catholic soon after the marriage, and bore four children. Mary, the first, was born on June 21, 1912, followed by Kevin, Preston, and Sheridan, "the only blond among us." Their family life, as it filters through to us through Mary McCarthy's memory, was extraordinarily happy and blessed. Her parents, she recalls, "were very much in love." Despite a continual state of debt Roy was a man "who insisted on turning everything into a treat." His daughter remembers that he was rarely in his law office in Seattle, more often in bed "entertaining us children." The writer in her recalls that he "was a romancer, and most of my memories of him are colored, I fear, by an untruthfulness that I must have caught from him. . . ." He and his beautiful (and also extravagant) wife made the children's lives unusually happy—full of glorious May baskets, picnics, Easter egg hunts, chocolate and cambric tea in the afternoons—so happy that contrast with the years that followed their parents' sudden death is all the more poignant. Mary McCarthy's world and the people in it became ugly, "cruel and inexplicable." The May flowers turned into sickly nasturtiums. Her golden age was prematurely over.

At six then, a terrible and impressionable age, the small girl had become an outsider. For the rest of her childhood, all of her adolescence, and much of her adult life this sense of being a stranger to the "in-groups" was to dominate her consciousness and, in time, to affect her choice of subject matter. I think it is undoubtedly true that it sharpened her mind, pointed her ambitions in the direction they took, and determined her satiric view. Three of her shorter works contain the same theme: the tightening of the ranks of "the residents" against the intruders, the establishment against the *arrivistes; The Group,* in its implied emphasis upon its own closed integrity, against the intrusion of the unqualified, "different" Kay, is a long, unspoken thesis, in one sense, against this kind of closed social organization.

In 1918 one of history's severest influenza epidemics swept the United States. The death of both Roy and Tess McCarthy in the epidemic was caused, in one sense, by "a decision . . . of the McCarthy family." Tired of the financial drain that the younger McCarthys made upon them (the prosperous Minneapolis grandparents were sending their invalid son and his family an allowance of almost a thousand dollars a month) they demanded that the young family move to Minneapolis "where my grandfather and grandmother could keep an eye on what was happening. . . ."

This event was contributory to the tragedy but not, of course, decisive. Uncle Harry, budding millionaire and white hope of the family, was sent to Seattle with his wife, Aunt Zula, to bring the family "home." They stayed at the best hotel in Seattle with the young McCarthys, who had sold their house in preparation for the move. Grandmother Preston was afterwards to claim that Harry and Zula "brought the flu with them." Whether or not this was so, the ill-fated expedition to Minneapolis started east in the fall of 1918. Aunt Zula and Sheridan were already sick. A week later Tess McCarthy, aged twenty-nine, was dead. The next day her husband, ten years her senior, died too. He had evaded the Prestons' direful prophecy "by taking my mother with him and leaving the question of the four children to be dealt with by his relatives."

At this point the lives of Mary McCarthy and her brothers take on the texture of soap opera. She has remarked on the improbability of real life in a critical essay, on the necessity of subduing actual events to make them believable. (Of a conference in Edinburgh in 1962 she said to the audience, "If I were to describe in a novel the conference . . . I would have to tone it down considerably to make it sound credible.") There is no doubt that memory of these improbable-sounding events may be colored, but the facts alone are shocking. "Yonder Peasant, Who Is He?," the opening chapter of her *Memories,* admittedly possesses "several dubious points," but if the details of this "angry indictment of privilege for its treatment of the underprivileged" are occasionally inaccurate there is no denying the authentic, if almost unbelievable, horror of its tone. In the five years that followed the children had experiences that seem to be plagiarized from Grimm or Charles Dickens. Mary, the child whose defining trait was "a passionate love of beauty," and her brother Kevin were submitted to a pair of guardians, a great-aunt and -uncle by marriage, Aunt Margaret and Uncle Myers, who had a "positive gift for turning everything sour and ugly." The rules of the household were odious and meaningless, the food plain and tasteless (after those unforgettable birthday cakes and ice-cream molds in the Seattle years), the discipline incredibly ingenious and harsh, their clothing darned and patched, their house ugly, the rooms dark and dingy. In the fiction of "Ghostly Father, I Confess," Meg remembers these days for the violence of the change, the opposites that set in at once; for the unhappy ending to the "pristine, fairly-tale period." As she lies on the psychiatrist's couch she thinks:

> Up to the time her mother had died, she had been such an elegant little girl. She remembered her ermine neckpiece and the ermine muff that went with it, her two baby rings with the diamonds in them, the necklace of seed pearls. All a little on the ostentatious side, she admitted, but it had been an era

> of bad taste. Then, after the flu was over, and mamma did not come home from the hospital, Aunt Clare had moved in, the rings were put in the vault (to keep for you until you're older), the ermine set wore out, the velocipede broke, the white sand darkened in the sandpile, there were prunes and rice pudding on the table, and the pretty little girl who looked (everybody said) so much like her mother was changed into a stringy, bowlegged child with glasses and braces on her teeth, long underwear, high shoes, blue serge jumpers that smelled, and a brown beaver hat two sizes too big for her.
>
> "*Ah,* she said to herself now, *I reject this middle-class tragedy, this degenerated Victorian novel where I am Jane Eyre or somebody in Dickens or Kipling or brave little Elsie Dinsmore fainting over the piano. I reject the whole pathos of the changeling, the orphan, the stepchild.*

What made these starved, colorless and miserable years even more poignant was the added contrast provided by the way of life of the wealthy grandparents McCarthy, two blocks away. To this haven of warmth, excellent cooking and spacious living, this "dwelling in sumptuous, middle-class style," Kevin and Mary often were returned when they ran away, were kept a blessed night and then promptly sent back to their Aunt Margaret and Uncle Myers in the morning.

What "saved" Mary in these years, she was later to admit, was religion—St. Stephen's School which she attended, and the Church to which it belonged:

> Our ugly church and parochial school provided me with my only aesthetic outlet, in the words of the Mass and the litanies and the old Latin hymns, in the Easter lilies around the altar, rosaries, ornamented prayer books, votive lamps, holy cards stamped in gold and decorated with flower wreaths and a saint's picture. This side of Catholicism, much of it cheapened and debased by mass production, was for me, nevertheless, the equivalent of Gothic cathedrals and il-

> luminated manuscripts and mystery plays. I threw myself into it with ardor, this sensuous life, and when I was not dreaming that I was going to grow up to marry the pretender to the throne of France and win back his crown with him, I was dreaming of being a Carmelite nun, cloistered and penitential; I was also much attracted by an order for fallen women called the Magdalens.

She was, as well, an excellent student, and her success at school was fostered by the competitive parochial system which, temporarily, and at the same time, maintained her religion:

> I stood at the head of my class and I was also the best runner and the best performer on the turning poles in the schoolyard; I was the best actress and elocutionist and the second most devout. . . . No doubt the standards of the school were not very high, and they gave me a false idea of myself; I have never excelled at athletics elsewhere. Nor have I ever been devout again. When I left the competitive atmosphere of the parochial school, my religion withered on the stalk.

At St. Stephen's Mary McCarthy's literary talent sprouted tentatively. "When I was eight, I began writing poetry at school: 'Father Gaughan is our dear parish priest/And he is loved from west to East.' " At ten her first real recognition came. Her brother Kevin tells that "she was bright . . . and there is the well-known story about winning first prize in a national essay contest when she was eleven. . . . When she came home our guardians beat her with a razor strop, so she wouldn't get uppity." He concludes that "something must have congealed right there within her breast against life as it is and as it has been."

Her version of the event is that, when she was ten, she wrote the essay, the facts for which she recalls taking directly from a series that was running in *Our Sunday Visitor*. She won first prize in the city, then the state prize; the award of twenty-five dollars was made at a school ceremony, and then confiscated by Uncle Myers as "much too good for her." It earned her as well "a razor strop across the bare bottom for special occasions, like the prize-winning."

The episode appears again in her fiction. The heroine of "Ghostly Father, I Confess" says to herself as she lies on the psychiatrist's blue couch: "I deny the afternoon I deliver my prize-winning essay at the Town Auditorium and there is no family there to applaud me because my father is away on a hunting trip, and my aunt, having just beaten me for my error in winning the prize ('You are too stuck-up already') is at home . . . having hysterics. . . ." In an episode of *Memories,* "A Tin Butterfly," ". . . my aunt was in the audience in her best mallard-feathered hat, looking, for once, proud and happy." And it is the uncle, not present, who at home "silently rose from his chair, led me into the dark downstairs lavatory . . . and furiously beat me with the razor strop—to teach me a lesson, he said, lest I became stuck-up. Aunt Margaret did not intervene."

Dickensian as all this is, and changed and transposed in minor details, the trauma of the event is still apparent. In reply to relatives who attributed her success as a writer to "the harsh formula followed in our upbringing," Mary McCarthy says: "Nor do I believe that artistic talent flowers necessarily from a wounding of the stem on which it grows."

The subject of the prize-winning essay was "The Irish in American History."

Like all stories replete with fairy-tale motifs, the evil-enchantment era of the McCarthy children's lives came to a "happy" end. Slowly, she thinks, the grandparents McCarthy "came to realize the true situation in our household," although in the five Grimm years they had never visited the orphans' household or checked to see how the funds they provided were being used (or "embezzled," as Mary McCarthy sometimes thought). They were possibly on the point of taking action when Grandfather Preston from Seattle arrived in Minneapolis and rescued them. The household was broken up almost immediately, Kevin and Preston went to their Grandfather McCarthy for a short stay during the summer vacation, and then were sent to school to St. Benedict's Academy in northern Minnesota. Sheridan later joined them there. Their winter vacations were spent at the boarding school; in the summer they visited relatives. Because of this solution to the problem of the orphans Mary McCarthy did not see her brothers again for six years, and when they met again "they were almost strangers." She went back west with her grandfather.

The two stories dealing with these "bad" years, "The Tin Butterfly" and "Yonder Peasant, Who Is He?," good reading as they are, are filled with highly connotative phrases and words: "poor orphans . . . raw hands and scarecrow arms . . . our elderly faces . . . my cruel uncle . . . stand in the snow, crying and beating sometimes on the window with our frozen mittens . . . our miserable clothes and underfed bodies." The effect is highly emotive, like the religious chromos the author emembers so poignantly, and so one finds oneself questionng the entire veracity of the memories. Does Mary McCarthy emember her early childhood in the primary colors of melodrama, as some critics have contended? The answer is, perhaps, to some extent, and if so her autobiography is an intersting exercise in fictionalization (or "characterization") of he truth, not departing from the core-fact but instead "handling" it as a novelist would, using careful choice, rerranging events, heightening the color or diminishing it, ouching up, and adding or subtracting details. Rejecting "the whole pathos of the changeling, the orphan, the stepchild," in one place, she herself recognizes that the condition itself is so highly connotative that it must be put aside for all practical (fictional?) purposes. In *A Charmed Life* John remarks about Dolly (the first of Mary McCarthy's orphans) that "an orphan . . . was just a figment who was sentimentalized by the whole world, like the heroine of a storybook; Dolly had never had any real privacy to develop herself in." And in "Ghostly Father," she states the poignancy of her recognition of the state herself: "Yet what were you going to do? You could not treat your life history as though it were an inferior novel and dismiss it. . . . Her peculiar tragedy (if she had one) was that her temperament was unable to assimilate her experience; the raw melodrama of those early years was a kind of daily affront to her skeptical, prosaic intelligence." Brock Brower has observed: "She would not have made a very good subject for an art novel; her life has been far too calamitous and outrageous."

Yet few writers in recent years have made such good use of autobiographical facts. Like a householder who puts every scrap of cloth or string or food to use, her autobiographical economy has been perfect; she seems to include in her fiction almost everything she remembers. If, in her use, she has "played" with the truth this is usually to the good. What results is not dreary, scrupulous, exact life history, but life history disseminated into all corners of the writer's products, autobiography as fiction, fiction drawing heavily upon autobiography.

One final digression: when a novelist resorts often to life history for material ("It is a case of lost identity. The author and the reader together accompany the heroine back over her life's itinerary," Mary McCarthy wrote), never moving too far from experience, family circle, acquaintances, husbands and lovers, like a novice swimmer reaching for a line she is reaching for *fact,* for the steadying rope, the hitching post of the actual, as if from distrust of the invented, the imagined, the conjured. This is one way of saying, and this point will be illustrated again and again, that Mary McCarthy's approach to fiction is that of the essayist, that the nucleus of truth or idea in her fiction is the essential element, and that her range of choice is limited to what is or was, only rarely including what might be.

Because I shall assert this point again let me explain the rather imprecise way I am using the word essayist. When I claim that Mary McCarthy is more of an essayist than a novelist I am making a distinction between the fictional impulse which starts with characters and works to develop, to deepen, and to bring, ultimately, to some end the *people* who are the essence of the work. Mary McCarthy's impulse, and that of a few other modern novelists, Jean-Paul Sartre and Albert Camus come to mind, is to begin with the *idée,* the thesis, and then (just as Montaigne studded his *Essais* —"attempts"—with pithy sayings and bits of classical wisdom) to use character to illustrate one or another aspect of the thesis. The result is almost an allegory ("The Young Man" and "The Young Woman" of "Cruel and Barbarous Treatment," the Realists and the Idealists of *The Oasis,* the girls of *The Group*), even more an essay, the thesis illustrated by character, the plot a simple proof, a demonstration of the point.

To return to what was. The rescuer of Mary McCarthy in 1923 was her grandfather Harold Preston, a Presbyterian Yankee. His father was Simon Manly Preston and his mother was a New England lady, Mary McCarthy's great-grandmother, whose name was Martha Sargent. It is of interest to note that this lady's first name was to serve her great-granddaughter for the heroine of *A Charmed Life* and her last name became the family name of the metamorphosing heroine of *The Company She Keeps,* Meg Sargent.

Harold Preston has been described by her as "a distinguished Seattle lawyer, former State Senator and local Bar Association president, framer of the first Workman's Compensation Act to be passed in the United States, an act which served as a model for later legislation. A conception of probity and public service was implanted in me by him, together with a certain legalistic temper." In "The Blackguard" he is described as "the most virtuous person I knew, whose name was a byword among his friends and colleagues for a kind of rigid and fantastic probity." Grandfather Preston brought the eleven-year-old Mary back to Seattle, and they were met at the depot by her grandmother, Gussie. A new and more fortunate phase of her polychrome life was to begin.

"He was not . . . thrifty," Mary McCarthy was to write later, "and I owe to his large-handedness and to an inheritance, later, from my other grandfather a very good education at Forest Ridge Convent in Seattle, at Annie Wright Seminary in Tacoma, and finally at Vassar College."

At Forest Ridge Convent, run by the Ladies of the Sacred Heart, she boarded for five days, came home on weekends. This was the school she had attended as a small child before leaving Seattle for Minneapolis. It was here upon her return that she heard a Jesuit sermon that caused her to worry about the eternal damnation of her grandfather's soul, became acquainted with Madame MacIllvra (the fictional name she gave to the real-life Madame McQueenie), the learned and liberal Mother Superior, and more enduringly, had words spoken to her by Madame Barclay (actually Madame Bartlett) that both stunned and flattered her and even, it might be, determined her course of future action. Madame Barclay, the English teacher, had been talking about Byron. That day she had written the words: *Zoe mou, sas agapo* (my life, I love you) on the board. Mary McCarthy could not bear this "democratization" of the poem she had learned by heart in her grandfather's library, so she ignored the teacher and began to draw pictures. "Suddenly the pointer cracked across my writing tablet. 'You're just like Lord Byron, brilliant but unsound,' " declared Madame Barclay. For Mary this was "a declaration of love," a "Don Juanesque triumph," and it was only diminished by her grandfather's horrified reception of the story. Madame Barclay had to make a public correction of her remark. She told her class that "Mary McCarthy did not resemble Lord Byron in any particular; she was neither brilliant, loose-living nor unsound." But if Madame Barclay recanted, her remark struck deep into the Byronic soul of her pupil, and her words often echo in critical attacks upon her. She is often to be called brilliant, attacked for loose living, and accused of fictional unsoundness.

At Sacred Heart Convent she studied "rhetoric, French, Literature, Christian doctrine, English history." Here she seems to have acquired her sense of history; "the past still vibrated in the convent." And here she "decided" to lose her faith, in order "to get myself recognized at whatever price." In *"C'est le Premier Pas Qui Coûte"* she tells the story of this event, which was not so much crucial and painful as it was accidental and willful:

> The truth is the whole momentous project simply jumped at me, ready-made, out of one of Madame MacIllvra's discourses. I had decided to do it before I knew what it was, when it was merely an interweaving of words, lose-your-faith, like a ladder made of sheets on which the daring girl had descended into the arms of her Romeo. "Say you've lost your faith," the devil prompted, assuring me that there was no risk if I chose my moment carefully. Starting Monday morn-

> ing, we were going to have a retreat, to be preached by a stirring Jesuit. If I lost my faith on, say, Sunday, I could regain it during the three days of retreat, in time for Wednesday confessions. Thus there would be only four days in which my soul would be in danger if I should happen to die suddenly. . . . If I did not do it, someone else might . . . It was a miracle that someone had not thought of it already, the idea seemed so obvious, like a store waiting to be robbed.

Having made her decision, having declared to the Mother Superior *"Ma Mère,* I have lost my faith," she was granted an interview concerning her "doubts" with Father Dennis (a fictional name). She managed to outfence the "old, dry, forbidding" priest ("I had always liked to argue with the clergy," she writes in "My Confession"), and in the act of dialectic she discovered that a genuine truth had been revealed to her: "there was no belief inside me." The act had become the reality, like that of a performer who forces a yawn on stage only to discover that he is genuinely tired.

With her faith, Mary McCarthy has written in fiction, she lost some of her sense of self, the part she had retained after the holocaust in which both parents died. Meg in "The Man in the Brooks Brothers Shirt" searches for someone who can tell her what she is really like, what her feelings really were. Meg thinks:

> Perhaps at last she had found him, the one she kept looking for, the one who would tell her what she was really like. . . . If she once knew, she had no doubt that she could behave perfectly; it was merely a question of finding out. How, she thought, can you act upon your feelings if you don't know what they are? As a little girl whispering to a young priest in the confessional she had sometimes felt sure. The Church could classify it all for you. . . . But when as a homely high-school girl, she had rejected the Church's filing system . . . she had given away her sense of herself.

This complete "loss" of faith ("I lost my faith very easily," she says in another place) was accompanied in these convent years by "practical" gains which she describes as her reasons for being glad she once was a Catholic:

> It gave me a certain knowledge of the Latin language and of the saints and their stories which not everyone is lucky enough to have. Latin, when I came to study it, was easy for me and attractive, too, like an old friend; as for the saints, it is extremely useful to know them and the manner of their martyrdom when you are looking at Italian painting.... To read Dante and Chaucer or the English Metaphysicals or even T. S. Eliot, a Catholic education is more than a help. ... If you are born and brought up a Catholic, you have absorbed a good deal of world history and the history of ideas before you are twelve ... the effect is indelible. Nobody else in America, no other group, is in this fortunate position. Granted that Catholic history is biased, it is not dry or dead; its virtue for the student, indeed, is that it has been made to come alive by the violent partisanship which inflames it.

After a brief spell in public school, Garfield High School in Seattle—her freshman year, during which she acquired a reciprocated interest in the other sex and during which, as a result, her grades declined sharply—her grandfather decided to transfer her to the Annie Wright Seminary, an Episcopal boarding school in Tacoma, "though I myself had wanted to go to the Anna Head School in California because Helen Wills had gone there."

Here she encountered Miss Ethel Mackay, called in *Memories of a Catholic Girlhood* Miss Harriet Gowrie, Scottish teacher of Latin, "black-haired ... tall, lean, [a] doll-jointed 'figger,' " who became a strong influence on her during three years at the Seminary. Miss Gowrie is the heroine of "The Figures in the Clock"; it was she who wrote the script and staged a memorable performance of *Marcus* ' *lius* in which Mary McCarthy played Catiline, the libert "the damned soul, proud and unassimilable, the mar gifted man." Her pleasure in the role is reminiscent of delight at Mother Barclay's coupling her with Byron, and almost the same reasons. This was, in addition, an early matic triumph, a taste of the delights of the art of acting were to be so seductive to her for many years. At the S nary, too, her love of Latin grew and with it its influ upon her prose style. She confesses that she "fell in love Caesar" under Miss Gowrie's teaching. "Latin came to very fluently . . . I felt as if I had known it in some o incarnation. Hence, writing with a Latinate turn, compres analytic, and yet having a certain extravagant or orato flourish, sounded in my ears like a natural spoken langua

"I was an ardent literary little girl," she writes in ano place, "getting up at four in the morning to write a se teen-page medieval romance before breakfast, smoking the fire-escape and thinking of suicide, meeting a crip boy in the woods by the cindery athletic field, composir novelette in study hall about the life of a middle-a prostitute. . . ."

The young "Catholic girl," as she may well have been scious of being, had some difficulties "being someone" at Episcopal school. Her grandparents were not in the Sea social swim, and so she belonged to no social set. She unsure now of what she was, even of her looks, and it be that her Catholic past had begun to bother her. She wr in "Ghostly Father, I Confess":

> The ugly duckling might be able to get along in life, adj resign itself, if there were not the charming, tantalizing sibility that at any moment it might turn into a swan. . . . that was what had happened. . . . The little girl

> looked like her mother had suddenly reappeared, seven years older, but otherwise unchanged. . . . She was pretty, she dressed expensively, she was gay, she made friends, and the only remarkable thing about her was that she had the air of coming from nowhere, of having no past. Her classmates in boarding school could not understand why they had never met her before. When they asked her about this, she would blush and say that her father had kept her in a convent. But this explanation was never quite adequate. "What about vacations?" they would wonder. "Who did you go around with?" "Oh, a lot of Catholic girls," she would answer. "It was very boring."

Her three years at Annie Wright were not without some early signs of rebellion and leadership. She ran away once, "just for fun," with another girl, she "did" things, like acting in school plays and becoming an officer of the French Club and the Latin Club. She recalls writing a number of "realistic" short stories and romances "rather in the manner of Maurice Hewlett," which she then took secretly to Miss Dorothy Atkinson, her much-admired English teacher, "for her private consumption." To offset all this early intellectualism she took a course in cooking "probably because the teacher was young and pretty; I was terrible at it." One summer she spent with some school friends in Montana; the wryly humorous results of that trip are the subject matter of "Yellowstone Park" in *Memories of a Catholic Girlhood.* Another, even more memorable one (when she was fourteen) was spent, like most other vacations from the Seminary, with her grandfather at Lake Crescent.

Graduation from Annie Wright was accomplished with another kind of Mary McCarthy flourish. Caught by Miss Gowrie coming in the gym window on her way back from meeting a boy, she equivocated to the principal—"I went out to smoke," she said—and thus broke rigid, upright Miss

Gowrie's heart. She was graduated with "triumphant salutes and valedictions," at the top of her class. Miss Gowrie did not return to the school—whether because her faith had been shattered or from some other cause, is not clear—but went "to Canada and Empire." Mary McCarthy prepared to go east to Vassar College.

Why did she decide to go to Vassar? She has offered two reasons, the first in "The Vassar Girl": ". . . the name, *Vassar,* entered my consciousness through the person of an English teacher. She symbolized to me the critical spirit, wit, cool learning, detachment—everything I suddenly wished to have and be. . . . The idea of going to Vassar and becoming like Miss A—— immediately dominated my imagination. . . . I tutored in Caesar during the summer and coaxed my family. To go east to college was quite a step in Seattle."

In conversation, Mary McCarthy has said that Miss Atkinson never talked about Vassar to her students. But it "was wanting to be like her" that made her think of going to Vassar. "We *knew* she was Vassar."

Or again, in the course of her long fictional search for self, her sense of having no easily recognizable history, she lets Meg Sargent suggest another reason. In "Ghostly Father, I Confess" she writes: "In a way, she supposed, it was to escape from these questions [concerning her history] that she had gone East to college. There, if you had money, and used the right fork, no one could suspect Aunt Clara in your vague but impeccable background." Substitute Minneapolis' Aunt Margaret for Aunt Clara and one comes close to Mary McCarthy's painfully honest summation of why she went to Vassar.

In the summer before she left Seattle, she studied dramatics at the Cornish School, a school she describes as an important cultural feature of Seattle life. Here she took a class with Ellen Van Volkenbergh Browne and remembers that Mark Tobey was also on the faculty. She learned "standard English pronunciation" as part of the school's required curriculum, took a class in eurhythmics which she loathed, and extended her cultural life to the concerts offered in Seattle Stadium. She says she "tried to grasp" the music she heard and utterly failed. Her interest was absorbed, rather, by the *names,* names connected with the sounds of the music, and she still remembers being fascinated with "sarabande" and "Scarlatti." It is notable that only infrequently in her subsequent fiction is there any indication that she has ever had any sort of taste for music although, as in this early memory, her ear for sounds when they are formulated into speech is excellent.

During that last summer in Seattle, and while she was going to drama school, she met her first husband-to-be, Harold Johnsrud, "what we then called my Dream Man." He was acting in the local little theatre, and had a part in a pageant about the Magna Carta put on for the Bar Association. In most ways the summer seems to have been "a sorry disappointment." The courses offered were unsatisfactory and she was given no speaking parts, appearing only as one of a chorus of underwater pirates. Daunted, but not completely discouraged in her theatrical ambitions, her hopes for a theatrical career were to revive somewhat in college.

Memories of a Catholic Girlhood contains a reproduction of a clipping from what appears to be the rotogravure section of a Seattle newspaper. "Miss McCarthy," the caption reads, "the granddaughter of Mr. and Mrs. Harold Preston, who left last week for the East to enter Vassar College." In the studio portrait of the seventeen-year-old Mary, she is glancing aside, her shining black hair pulled tight to the back of her head in what is to be her single, consistent style of coiffure for many years, and her characteristic smile is restrained into an almost crooked, upward motion. She is, it would seem, trying to smile without much success, at something. Or else it is that she has just smiled her characteristic, wide grin, flashed it once brilliantly, and exhausted it. There is also a picture of her in "her neat cloche hat and careful little traveling suit." She looks young, Irish, innocent and charming. Only in that curious, crooked smile is there a trace of the land-pirate, the "critical spirit" to be.

* * *

Mary McCarthy stopped off in Minneapolis in the fall of 1929 on her way to matriculate at Vassar. Grandmother McCarthy's friend, Father Cullen, had been invited to the house "to back up" her view that Vassar was " 'a den of iniquity.' " Father Cullen refused to agree and instead told Mary "of the rare intellectual opportunities Vassar had in store for me." Much later in "The Vassar Girl" she tells the story again, that her grandmother "sent for the parish priest to armor me against the 'heresy' I should be exposed to. The priest was . . . embarrassed . . . contented himself with a few rumbling remarks about the efficacy of prayer and the sacraments, and then admonished the old lady that at Vassar I would find the very best of Western thought, contemporary and classical—I ought to be proud to be going there. . . . I hardly knew whether to be more thrilled by the priest's liberal commendation or by my grandmother's conservative disapproval." This must have been Mary McCarthy's last encounter with her grandmother's "bloodcurdling Catholicism"; the next time she passed through on her way to college both grandparents had died, her brothers were now living with a new guardian, Uncle Louis, and a chapel in Texas had been erected in her grandmother's name with money left for that purpose in her will.

Once arrived in the East, Mary McCarthy, her grandmother and her aunt spent some time in New York before the college year began. In what seemed like Fate to her, she met Harold Johnsrud again; he was the only person she knew in New York. She had gone with her relatives to visit the Metropolitan Museum of Art, and her aunt insisted on seeing the American Wing. In Mary's "haste and aesthetic fury" she escaped from them, fell down the whole Metropolitan staircase, started for her hotel, and met Johnsrud in the street. Shortly afterwards their affair began and was to culminate, with only a short hiatus when he went to Hollywood in 1932 to work as a scriptwriter for MGM, in their marriage in June 1933. Her memory of the years of her affair with him is that it was intensely painful. Johnsrud seemed to enjoy his power over the young Vassar girl; his letters were full of references to other women he encountered, lurid descriptions of call girls, all purportedly secondhand. This she doubted and was, it may well be, cruelly hurt by it all.

The four college years, like her encounter with Catholicism, were definitive for her work. It is safe to say that no one in current literature has made better, more widespread, more complete and detailed use of the experiences of a college education, both in its particulars and its generalities, than Mary McCarthy. Thirty years later her memories of the college at Poughkeepsie were to serve her as the basis for her first best seller, *The Group*. They were to provide her with an occasion earlier, in 1951, for a piece in *Holiday,* "The Vassar Girl," which represented the fruits of a return visit to the campus to assess the college eighteen years after her graduation. Two years after that she used Vassar again for background material which appears in the beginning portions of her political essay, "My Confession," and perhaps the academic atmosphere in her novel, *The Groves of Academe,* was touched here and there by her own academic memories. Over and over again, Mary McCarthy's heroines are heavily dependent for backgrounds on references to their college years. Dolly and Martha in *A Charmed Life* "went to college together"; Meg in "The Man in the Brooks Brothers Shirt" had "gone East to college" from Portland, Oregon. In a later story in *The Company She Keeps* the particular place in the "east" becomes the dream locale of "Eggshell College" where "there was a sort of outing cabin." Like their author, a good number of McCarthy heroines are college women who have been irrevocably touched by their college experience as much as, or more than, by their formal college education. Like Mary McCarthy they do not easily recover from those years, if indeed they ever do, although more often than not they (unlike their author) fail to be educated in the academic sense by their experience.

Her four years at Vassar extended her classical education begun at the convent and at Annie Wright Seminary. She says that she "pursued her early interest in the classics. . . . I graduated from Vassar in 1933 full of Juvenal and Martial, Catullus, Shakespeare, Nashe and Greene." Besides classical and Elizabethan writers she acquired a taste for criticism, an unfeminine sharpness of attack more characteristic of Rome or the English eighteenth-century essayists than of American women writers of the twentieth century. Elizabeth Hardwick has remarked that Mary McCarthy is closer in spirit to Margaret Fuller than to any other American woman writer. And at Vassar this critical mind, which she was later to question ("I had been terribly discouraged when I was at Vassar . . . by being told that I was really a critical mind and that I had no creative talent"), was apparently given its head. The cutting edge of her mind sharpened in these four years was later, in *The Group,* to turn against its hone. A classmate is reported to have said about her college years: "She was extremely intolerant; in class, her criticisms were merciless."

Early in her freshman year she began a career as a literary person. For Freshman English (105) she produced this prose, which was chosen by the faculty for inclusion in its publication, *The Sampler*. It was entitled *Contrasts:*

I.

THE HOUSE OF GOD

The church was quiet with reverence, and dim with holiness. Far down at the altar, tall tapers burned ardently, but they did not disturb the still twilight of God's house. There a priest moved slowly back and forth, repeating the solemn words of the most sacred Mass. His voice was low, and rightly so, but now and again a phrase drifted down from the altar. "Dominus vobiscum." One could feel the Divine Presence hovering over the altar, enveloping it and the intent worshipers. The Priest and the altar-boys were feeling it and chanting of it; their dark-red robes were symbolic of the richness of God's grace; the incense they burned, of the sweetness of His love.

Near the front of the church, a window was open. Beyond it was a patch of blue sky, and the green branch of an apple-tree waving in the wind. They, too, were expressing the ineffable goodness of God. All life, human and inanimate, bowed down to Him, and was bathed in His peace.

II.

A SURVIVAL

Outside the open church window there is spring. The sky is an intense blue. The green branch of an apple-tree waves gently in the wind.

Inside there is gloom and unreality; inside, there is a priest. Around a shadowy altar, a few feeble tapers burn. Grey wisps of incense salute a God, old beyond human un-

> derstanding. A book is moved back and forth on the altar by small, puzzled boys. Their robes are like those of the priest, dark red, the red of old blood and time-worn sacrifices. A few Latin words drift down toward the worshipers, dead ritual, in a dead language to a dead God. A thin piece of whitish bread is raised; and the believers bow their heads and beat their breasts in fear and adoration.
>
> The spring and the sky and the apple tree seem more breathtakingly real as the grotesque mummery is enacted far in the front of the church. But one notices that the spring shrinks from the open window; it remains very definitely outside, as the weary mutterings of a sacred Mass go on.

In startling contrast to the emotional tone of these freshman efforts Mary McCarthy produced in her senior year a sixteen-page research paper for English 463 (Studies in the English Renaissance) which was printed in the *Vassar Journal of Undergraduate Studies.* Signed Mary Therese McCarthy (a name under which she is still often catalogued by libraries) the term paper, "Touchstone Ambitious" is a notably well-written piece of student research, a study of Sir John Harington, Queen Elizabeth's godson. He was termed "the merry poet," one who was early infected with "itching ambition," but whose affection for a "scurvy jest" and whose tendency to write "travestie" doomed his ambitions. One of his major accomplishments, one learns from the paper, was a treatise, *The Metamorphosis of Ajax,* a humorous and comprehensive study of the privy based upon Harington's own invention of a water closet.

His difficulties with the Tudor establishment seem to have started early. Mary McCarthy quotes a letter written to him as a young man by his cousin, Robert Markham:

> I say, do you not meddle in any sorte, nor give your jesting too freely among those you know not . . . I say this that your own honestie may not shew itself too muche . . . Stifle your

> understandinge as much as may be; mind your bookes, and make your jestes, but take heed who they light on.

More noteworthy even than the paper itself, which is early evidence of the scholar and critic to come, is her choice of subject. ("It would have been quite in Miss Sandison's style to have assigned us *The Metamorphosis of Ajax,* but I don't think she did.") For John Harington shared with Mary McCarthy two characteristics: frankness at all costs, and an overpowering need to speak his own mind. But Harington's honesty later gave way before his ambition, before his ability to change his coat, to seek royal favor. Here the stern-eyed young Elizabethan student cannot help showing her disdain. Ambition had "deflected his talent," and this was (witness her later attacks upon American playwrights especially) in her eyes the unforgivable sin.

"Real" references to Vassar abound in her fiction, notably in *The Group.* "Old Miss Washburn," Hallie Flanagan and "Lester," Miss Beckwith's Folklore course, Miss Peebles, Miss Kitchel's English 105, Miss Rindge, Miss Lockwood's contemporary press course, "old Miss McCurdy, the head of the Greek department" and Miss Sandison—all of these make it clear that, even thirty years later, the women who taught Mary McCarthy and the courses they taught were perfectly remembered by her. When Norine says that she belonged to an "out-group . . . the politicals . . . you people were the aesthetes . . . you were Sandison. We were Lockwood . . . Kay was Flanagan . . . Priss was Newcomer . . . Lakey was Rindge," she is satirizing a way of thinking that Mary McCarthy shared with her fellows at college, a way of identifying with the stream of ideas and behavior that the *person* of the college instructor represented, as well as the ideas themselves. The absolute imprint of these persons as teachers upon the minds and memories of their pupils is somewhat startling. She speaks again of Norine's distinctions in "The Vassar Girl": "The Socialists made friends with us, though they swore by Miss Lockwood's press course, and we by Miss Sandison's Renaissance or by Miss Rindge's art [course] or by a course in Old English or in verse writing: our group, being aesthetes, was naturally more individualistic."

These *Group* allusions make clear as well the influence of the maiden-lady professors, later to be referred to as the *emeritae,* upon the young Mary McCarthy. It was both what they taught and what they *were* that impressed her. As she was later to express regret at the passing of the iconoclastic, individualistic Vassar student like "Inez Mulholland, '09, who rode a white horse down Fifth Avenue campaigning for woman suffrage" so too does she acknowledge a deep and enduring affection (in "The Vassar Girl," written in 1951, if not in quite the same terms in *The Group*) for the type of woman college professor now departed from the campus scene. She remembers "the idea of excellence, the zest for adventure, the fastidiousness of mind and humanistic breadth of feeling... a certain largeness of mind, an amplitude of style, the mantle of a calling, a sense of historical dignity" that she feels these women possessed. These rolling phrases evoke an ideal that is to weave itself in and out of her subsequent thinking and into her fiction. At Vassar—at least in retrospect—she carried on her admiration of Miss Atkinson of Annie Wright Seminary and of Madame Bartlett of Sacred Heart Convent, of the woman scholar, proud and solitary, somewhat detached and romantic, undisturbed by the base calling of sex, a stern woman accomplished and objective. The ideal of the *emeritae* is to become as much a part of Mary McCarthy's system of values (and her fiction) as Elizabethan drama and classical poetry. It is best personified in a single real figure, Miss Sandison, the most constantly invoked of all the Vassar ladies, "slight, gray-haired, pretty Helen Sandison, the Elizabethan specialist, like an Elizabethan heroine herself, with her mettlesome sharpness, her hatred of imprecision and of bowdlerization of texts . . . fired with the ardor of teaching and capable of all the renunciations that the unmarried teacher who lives with a few books and prints in a faculty dormitory must make." (Recently, asked about Miss Sandison, the Vassar girl of thirty-three years ago replied: "Oh yes, Miss Sandison. An idol of mine still.") In *The Group* Helena says that "lots of women can live without sex and thrive on it. Look at our teachers in college. They weren't dried up or sour." Mrs. Renfrew, advising Dottie in the same book to make sacrifices for love, holds the *emeritae* up as examples: "Look at your teachers, look what they gave up."

This admiration will be found in other places, in somewhat different terms. In an interview in *Vogue* just before the publication of *The Group,* Mary McCarthy said that she preferred the *mothers* of the Vassar girls to the girls themselves. The mothers were "large figures from the past, and the girls are sitting on their ample laps like little girls on the lap of a great big madonna. . . . The mothers sort of belong to the full suffragette period with its great amplitude—you know, women smoking cigarettes in holders and dancing the cha-cha—and the girls are rather tinny in comparison with the mothers, I'm afraid." The woman of strength, independence, and amplitude is her heroine, and she always seems to be a collage of Miss Atkinson, Madame Bartlett, and the revered Miss Sandison.

By senior year, as already noted, the maturation of her style and subject matter was evident. She and a group of English majors began a publication of their own, in revolt against the existent *Review,* which they declared in their first editorial did not publish "any forward-looking writing because it aims to represent the majority of the college." Suggesting that there must be a place in the literary life of the college for this "pathetic minority" who wrote forward-looking writing, the publication, *Con Spirito* (named by Elizabeth Bishop), first appeared in February 1933. The anonymous editors paid for its publication themselves.

> We had a rebel literary magazine that Elizabeth Bishop and Eleanor Clark were on, and Muriel Rukeyser and I. I wrote, not fiction, but sort of strange things for this publication... there was an official literary magazine which we were all against. Our magazine was anonymous. It was called *Con Spirito.* It caused a great sort of scandal. I don't know why—it was one of those perfectly innocent undertakings.... *Con Spirito* lasted for only a few numbers.

One of Mary McCarthy's contributions was a prose poem with poetic interpolations which she called *"In Pace Requiescamus."* The form was somewhat confused, the product of the then-popular approach to style called "automatic writing." It dealt, "in a mixed-up way, with the Polish Corridor and the Jews." It grew out of "a flurry of indignation," against Mussolini and Italian fascism, against Hitler and the Nazis, against Pope Pius XII and his irrelevant birth-control encyclicals, his inane activity of setting "new red hats on his prelates' bald heads" while Jews were being beaten and the threat of extinction by bombing grew daily greater. The tone of the piece is fury. It is remarkable mainly for its schoolgirl's prescience, its awareness of danger and the coming shape of things, as far back as the April 1933 issue of *Con Spirito.*

Stemming from Vassar were other McCarthy attitudes. Characterizing the Vassar girl in a later essay, "My Confession," she notes that a Vassar girl possesses "the passion for public service coupled with a yearning for the limelight, a wish to play a part in the theatre of world events. . . ." This passion for the limelight, this sense her heroines have that they are both *being* and acting, watching themselves play roles within the action of the novel is, one suspects, Mary McCarthy's own. The "She" in *The Company She Keeps* is a case of this; by the kind of extension from self to fiction that she makes constantly, the tendency to playacting in their lives becomes Meg Sargent's, Martha Sinnott's, Kay Strong's.

Speaking more generally of the Vassar girl she sees her as possessing "a wistful respect for the unorthodox." And "Vassar has a peculiar power of conveying a sense of excellence." In both sentences Mary McCarthy suggests her own discernible gains from college. In her discussion of the "rebel literary magazine" one senses others: an admiration, even a positive bent, for the rebellious, an uncontrollable desire to be an iconoclast and then, notable in many of Mary McCarthy's later utterances, an astonished dismay at the effects of this attitude on others. "It caused a great scandal—I don't know why": the naïve note in this is to be repeated again and again whenever, in the course of her writing life, she is to shock, surprise or hurt. This professed, childlike amazement at the "way" people take what she says or what she writes is first heard in her words about the scandalized reception of the Vassar literary magazine. One begins to wonder about its genuineness when one remembers the care with which the twelve-year-old Mary planned to shock the nuns and priests with her loss of faith. There would seem to be a complex of motives and acts—the desire to play an unusual part for its effect on others, and then the expression of innocent surprise at the result. She herself makes no attempt to explain her curious naïveté. When asked, "How do you account for it?" she is likely to throw up her hands and respond, "Just stupidity, I guess."

At Vassar Mary McCarthy was allied with the party of the aesthetes. "I was very apolitical in college," she confessed. "My official political philosophy was royalism . . . my real interests were literary. . . . I really hated absolutism and officiousness of any kind (I preferred my kings martyred)." This apoliticalism (modified, she admits, by her interest in the fate of the Jews in Germany and a certain "disturbing" concern for the Sacco-Vanzetti and Tom Mooney cases) was to disappear after Vassar; the aestheticism, somewhat transformed into a transcendent concern for literary style, persisted and strengthened itself in later years.

Finally, it is clear that despite the intellectual gains to her personally, and the general advantages of a Vassar education that are extolled in "The Vassar Girl," *The Group* contains some of her more mature thinking on the subject of a college education for the small Group in the novel: for them it had very little, almost no value at all. Critics in general have avoided this point, but the truth seems to be that the eight girls are not the heroines of *The Group,* nor is there one conglomerate heroine made up of the eight faces, as Diana Trilling has suggested. Nor are the men to any significant degree the villains. Heroine and villain are Vassar, the common spawning ground of the eight girls. It is to Vassar they constantly return in their thoughts, Vassar is the source of their allusions, the meat of their conversations. It determines their subsequent behavior and affects their values, or does nothing to modify the values they brought with them. Vassar gives form to their decisions in later life (or at least seven years after graduation it still does); they return to it mentally for advice, sustenance and a sense of security. The girls consider that Kay "had been amazingly altered" by a course in Animal Behavior she had taken with old Miss Washburn; Priss knows about "expatriates and bohemian rebels" because of Miss Lockwood's press course; Dottie's night of defloration takes place on "Midsummer's night, the summer solstice, when maids had given up their treasure to fructify the crops"; she knew that and was able fortunately to make the correct reference at the right time because she "had it" at Vassar in her background reading for *A Midsummer Night's Dream*. However, Krafft-Ebing, which she and Kay and Helena had read in college, fails Dottie in the same scene: she wishes "books were a little more explicit." When Dick tells Dottie to "get yourself a pessary" it is to her college course in zoology that she at once refers. "A vision of a coarse piglike mammal they had studied in Zoology" provides her with a vision of a "peccary." And when she looks at Dick, disheveled and smiling cruelly, he reminds her of "Hamlet—of course—putting Ophelia away from him . . . (which was the most pathetic moment in the whole play, the class had decided"). What these women think and remember depends to a large extent on what they did at Vassar, indeed on the fact they *were* at Vassar. Group values and subsequent group sentiments expressed by the individual in postgraduate life were all nurtured in the Tower suite of Main. The impression of "what they learned at Vassar" is so intense to the girls that if the reader were acute he might be able to predict Lakey's lesbianism, only revealed at the end of the novel, in chapter one when Dottie, in bed with Dick that first night, hears herself pretend to tell him: "One of the older teachers told Lakey that you have to live without love, learn not to need it, in order to live *with* it. Lakey was terrifically impressed. . . ." Lakey's sexual fate is, in this way, almost determined at Vassar by the words of "the older teacher."

At moments of greatest trial or decision it is to Vassar and to memories of Vassar that the girls turn for guidance. In the doctor's office Kay, who is observing everything minutely, recalls that " 'extend your antennae, girls' was a favorite apothegm of the teacher she had respected most." When Harald tells Kay about being fired she reminds herself to get the whole truth of his story, "not just his own partial view of it. That was the big thing they taught you at Vassar: keep your mind open and always ask for the evidence even from your own side." Again, Kay is depressed ("because of her heavy legs and the hairs scattered on them") in the presence of a New York actress, and not at all consoled by the memory that comes to her "that she had directed a Hall Play and been on the Daisy Chain at Vassar."

It is not only that the thoughts and conversation of the Group are full of such retrospective references; it is also that their *ways* of thought are attributable by Mary McCarthy totally to Vassar. Their judgments have been formulated there, their later behavior determined by the college. Libby talks to the young editor, Mr. Leroy: " 'All work ought to be interesting. Even manual labor. Hear, hear!' she added jovially, in the manner she had learned at Vassar." Running into translation problems while book-reviewing for a liberal weekly, her inclination is to dash up "to Vassar to consult Mr. Roselli but, woe was her, he was on sabbatical leave. . . ." The curious thing about this "thought" of Libby's is that she has been graduated from Vassar and in New York for two years when it occurs to her, yet her mind returns unerringly to thoughts of Vassar for help. Even more curious is the fact that she knows the whereabouts of faculty members after all this time. Polly, too, still thinks in terms of Vassar: after three years in New York she still considers herself "a science major."

Other people feel the need to make members of the Group comfortable by reference to their college. Mr. Leroy says: "Miss Chambers, who's been with us twenty years. I think she was Vassar too." Polly's landlady was "actually" Vassar, class of '18; Gesell's daughter (Norine places his work by this reference) was '35; at Kay's wedding, which begins *The Group,* Priss interprets the toast to the class of '33 by "the radio man" as evidence that "Vassar girls, in general, were not liked . . . by the world at large; they had come to be a sort of symbol of superiority." Vassar is mother, Bible, church and counsellor to its graduates, Vassar is Mecca, Elysium, Eden, obsessing their thoughts, crowding their field of reference; it has a monopoly on what they have learned, what they know, and (this must be a major part of Mary McCarthy's point in this novel) it limits what they are capable of learning in the future.

Clearly, of course, Mary McCarthy is talking here about what she observed in a limited group of her classmates, not in herself. She was later to remind an interviewer that she was *not* studying exceptional girls. She is wryly critical of the Vassar girls in *The Group,* of their inability to change, to progress intellectually and psychically beyond Taylor Gate, to remain immune to faddish thought. That she herself moved successfully far beyond, to Florence, to Paris, to Wellfleet and Stamford, to Venice and to Edinburgh, to international politics and the worlds of the theatre, literary criticism, art history and the novel, there is no doubt. However, just as the earnest little Catholic girl, wounded by a Dickensian childhood, lurks behind much that she writes, so the Vassar girl, '33, is the critic and judge of society behind the arras of a wider and more worldly approach. "He was more intelligent than she was, but he had not had a Vassar education," Polly thinks as she tries to decide about marrying Jim. The fulcrum is the Vassar education, for Polly, Kay, Dottie and all the others. It is, more often than she realizes, for Mary McCarthy too.

It is curious that Mary McCarthy, who got more mileage out of her college experience than any other American fiction-writer in memory, has never maintained a single formal tie with her college. The familiar phrase, "I was Vassar——" rings in her writing but not in her actions or speech. From the day she left Poughkeepsie in 1933 until her return visit at *Holiday*'s behest eighteen years later, she only occasionally returned to the place. She is remembered by her classmates as she was in 1929-1933 (and it should be noted that these memories were gathered after *The Group* appeared), as an intense girl with "a skinny figure," a harsh, angular hair-do, who scared them with her brains, raced about the campus in flat shoes, strands of hair out of place and a look, one classmate remembers, of "a sort of beatnik–unwashed, unbrushed, sort of gray." Mary McCarthy's reaction to these remarks is to doubt that these classmates knew her, since one of her oddities "was always wearing high heels, at the very least, Cuban." Some of her contemporaries recall with pleasure that she was not on the Daisy Chain; her class yearbook reveals that they completely ignored her when it came to choosing outstanding members of the class for notice. She was neither The Prettiest, The Best-Dressed, The Brightest, or The Most Likely to Succeed, nor anything else in that customary list. Only one classmate (at least in print) recalls her with something like compassion and admiration. Now a practicing psychiatrist, she remembers that Mary McCarthy was "aloof, independent, irrelevant . . . lonely," seemingly rootless because she, unlike most of the others, had no real family she had to please. "She appeared to be much freer than we were and this fascinated and frightened us."

She was one of the first, like Kay Strong of *The Group* who has so much of her author in her, to "run around the long table" on Class Day, "which meant you were announcing your engagement to the whole class." Like Kay she was the first girl of '33 to marry. She never went back to a class reunion, to the intense relief of her classmates who confessed that "we were terrified of her sarcasm." But she continued to see a few of them, notably the literary ones on the rebel magazine she helped to start, and the roommates of her Group who were eventually to find pieces and parts of themselves resurrected in the novel.

II *The Partisan Reviewer*

INTERVIEWER: *Do you now consider yourself a novelist?*

MMcC: *Yes. Still, whatever way I write was really, I suppose, formed critically.*

ARMED with "the Vassar education," a Phi Beta Kappa key, her instant, engaging smile and a growingly acid and distrustful mind, Mary McCarthy went to New York in 1933. She had only recently (and reluctantly) abandoned the idea of being an actress. She recalls that, after playing Leontes in *A Winter's Tale* in her senior year, "an actor I later married came to see my performance and told me the truth: I had no talent. I gave up the dream that had been with me thirteen years . . . I started to write instead, which did not interest me nearly so much, chiefly because it came easier." The ambition she had held passionately until twenty-one had to be given up. She later told an interviewer humorously, "My tragedy was that I became a writer instead." Or the decision may have been due not so much to Harold Johnsrud's brutal frankness as to her own choice of pleasures. Meg Sargent reveals of herself in "Cruel and Barbarous Treatment": "She doubted whether she could ever have been an actress, acknowledging that she found it more amusing and more gratifying to play herself than to interpret any character conceived by a dramatist." However, she says that this thought of Meg's is pure fiction and not autobiographical at all. One week after graduation, on June twenty-first, her birthday, she married her critic, the actor and playwright, Harold Johnsrud.

After four troubled years, during which her affection for him went through a good many vicissitudes, Mary McCarthy's affair with Johnsrud, terminated surprisingly, in marriage. Her recollection now is that not only did she never quite know "why he finally decided to marry me," but that also she herself was no longer, at that point, very eager for marriage. "My power of suffering had been exhausted by him," she now says. It is possible that her agreement to marry him was purely a decision of convention. There was prestige among the Group in being the first married and like Kay, "the iconoclast and scoffer" of *The Group,* to be married was the only thing now left to do, after the long and much-publicized affair. At all events, they married, on a day and at a ceremony of which the first chapter of *The Group* may very well be a close approximation.

Johnsrud was "in some ways very much like me. He was the son of a Minnesota Normal School administrator who had been the scapegoat in an academic scandal. . . . My husband brooded over his father's misfortunes, like Hamlet or a character in Ibsen, and this had given his nature a sardonic twist." His appearance was somewhat strange—bald, a broken nose, a "tense, arresting figure"—and kept him from achieving much variety as an actor. He was a member of the Theatre Union, a left-wing group of players, he did some playwriting and some directing; he acted in *Winterset, Key*

Largo, and other plays. "In personal life he was very winning," is Mary McCarthy's summary statement about her first husband; he comes to our notice in modified form as the major male character in *The Group.*

His significance to Mary McCarthy's career is somewhat humorous. She claims that her marriage to Johnsrud qualified her for an early job as drama critic on *Partisan Review,* one she held sporadically for ten years beginning in 1937, after her divorce from the actor. "The field assigned to me was the theatre, because, just before this, I had been married to an actor." And in another place: "I had been married to an actor, and so was supposed to know something about the theatre." The humor of this *non sequitur* appealed to her, the element of irrationality and accident that it represents as well are to recur in her career.

As the prototype for Harald Petersen of *The Group* he seems to me to be the figure to whom Mary McCarthy attached much of what she then thought, and later was to say, about husbands, marriage, careers, men, and sex, successful and unsuccessful. Harald (the name change in the novel is minor but accounted for by "that was the way he spelled it, the old Scandinavian way") was a "thin, tense young man," with black straight hair who had once tried "during exam week" to commit suicide "by driving somebody's car off a cliff." He is intelligent yet stupid in personal relations, cynical, selfish, unfaithful; he loses his job in a way that throws suspicion upon his character and his virility; he is weak, scornful of the Group. ("God's bowels, how tired I was of the Group before I was through," he declares at the end of the novel, and to Lakey, as he climbs out of her car on the way to bury Kay, he says: "You bury her, you and the Group.") He lacks decisiveness, he is often vicious and, like Harold Johnsrud, he had "Scandinavian fits of bitter depression," during which "he was still fighting his father's battles," his father who "had been principal of the high school in Boise" and then "made an enemy of the vice-principal, who brought about his dismissal." Kay worries that Harald may be reliving his father's pattern of failure; both men seemed to be weak, and to have an episode of conspiracy in their parental backgrounds. There is a good deal of Mary McCarthy in Kay, and Kay's husband, Harald, is not unlike Harold Johnsrud in many ways.

The marriage to Johnsrud lasted three years. She and Johnsrud lived on Beekman Place, moved among the Village intellectuals, and went to left-wing parties where they drank a great deal. In these years Mary McCarthy's political awareness increased; she says she abandoned her royalist views in the light of her new acceptance of "the need for social reform," and her new awareness "of Communists as a distinct entity." There was no specificity in her new feelings. She was like Meg in "Portrait of the Intellectual as a Yale Man," who is asked, " 'Is it true you are a Trotskyite?' The girl shook her head. 'I'm not even political.' " In an interview in 1963 Mary McCarthy said: "I never took a very active part, I was more or less passive, I got involved with politics because the men I was with were involved in politics, and I was just there . . . I was less interested in ideas at that time. I think I was much more of a literary girl . . . it was only the Moscow trials, I think, that put my mind to work."

The couple's attitude toward the Communist Party was "not hostile but merely unserious," an attitude that was to characterize her political tone for some time: unserious, uncommitted and, in addition, subject to accident. The essay, "My Confession," tells of her and her husband's tentative, fringe contacts with the Party, a bit of marching in the May Day parade, a few debates, some picketing, going "once or twice to a class for actors in Marxism, just to see what was up." At the time Mary McCarthy was writing book reviews for *The Nation* ("somewhat iconoclastic," she remembered them as being) and doing other free-lance work: "I used to do research and typing for a disgruntled, middle-aged man," later identified as Benjamin Stolberg, who was a violent critic of the Party. She tells of a cocktail party at which James Farrell, "dimple-faced, shaggy-headed, earnest," asked her if she didn't think Trotsky was entitled to a hearing? Her ignorance of just what Trotsky had done was profound; she had been away in Seattle and Reno during the months of the Moscow trials and had heard nothing about them. She inquired and was told. In her confusion she wondered: "Were there people who would say that Trotsky was *not* entitled to a hearing?" Later she was to tell an interviewer: "I got swept into the whole Trotskyite movement. But by accident." This innocent blunder, or rather, this naïve insistence upon principle without knowledge of the harsh political realities behind it, of which she was unaware, ended in her finding her name on the letterhead of the Committee for the Defense of Leon Trotsky. Her horror at the realization that the Trotskyites had helped themselves to her signature was mitigated somewhat by her dislike of being "warned" by the Communists (as she was), and by her fastidious distaste at joining the "sorry band" of publicly announced defectors from the letterhead list who had yielded to the pressure tactics of the Communists. With this act, which was both negative and the result of delay (she had *intended* indignantly to retract her name but "had been saved" by neglecting to do so) Mary McCarthy became known as an anti-Communist. She felt toward the Communists much as she had felt toward the convent priests: she resented their authoritarianism, unreason, and pressure. And it is possibly true that much of what she is she seems to have been made by reaction to pressures brought to bear against her. Retreating from them, she stumbles into "a kind of" conviction, the nature of which is often defined by the action of accident and chance in her experiences. She herself is aware that her anti-Communism is "the result of chance and propinquity."

One other reason for her Trotskyism is suggested in her story, "The Genial Host." Pflaumen, the host of the title, describes Meg Sargent to his dinner guests, and Meg thinks to herself: "It was just that you were temperamentally attracted to unpopular causes: when you were young, it had been the South, the Dauphin, Bonnie Prince Charlie; later it was Debs and now Trotsky that you loved. You admired this romantic trait in yourself. . . ." The romantic lover of lost causes, the Byronic heroine, is true Mary McCarthy. In addition, Meg thinks, this affection for Trotsky "was just another way of showing off, of setting yourself apart from the run of people." The actress, the intellectual, the romantic, and the girl who became interested in politics because the men around her were, the product of accident and chance, this catalogue explains Mary McCarthy's conversion from girlhood royalism to the world of serious political thought.

Even before graduation she had applied for a job at *The New Republic*. She was "not drawn there by the magazine's editorial policy—I hardly knew what it was—but because the book-review section seemed to me to possess a certain elegance and independence of thought that would be hospitable to a critical spirit like me." In her first winter in New York, and following her marriage, her literary career began. She wrote reviews of novels and biographies for *The New Republic* and *The Nation*, despite the "nervous guilt" she confesses to have felt as she passed through the magazines' waiting rooms and saw the "shabby young men who were waiting too." Her guilt was for her own chic, well-dressed bourgeois self in contrast to their "poor, pinched" look, and for her relative indifference to politics beside their "busy social conscience." Her reviews were sharp, merciless, unsympathetic to weak thinking and poor writing, iconoclastic. Early victims were Hilaire Belloc, Glenway Wescott, Eric Linklater, Philip Wylie, Kay Boyle, James Hilton, Mary Ellen Chase, and a host of more minor figures.

At about this time too, beginning in 1935, she published, in collaboration with Margaret Marshall (then associate editor of *The Nation*) a series of articles on literary critics, articles which are very much in the familiar tone of her subsequent critical work. From the practicing critics' point of view they were harsh and uncharitable; pointed sharply to the weaknesses, foolishness, and ineptitude of critics, they suggested the very real injustices that stupid but compassionate critics committed against the public by recommending second-rate, weak-minded pap and ignoring really excellent work.

These five articles begin by stabbing away at the wide field of practicing book critics and their "critical tomfoolery." True, they are written in collaboration, but their sound and fury are almost surely the characteristic tone of the young literature major, the land wrecker, two years out of college. She has elsewhere (in "Yonder Peasant, Who Is He?") confessed her awareness of her own egoism; combined with an inviolable and youthful conviction of her own rectitude, and her early-developed incapacity to say anything she does not believe, these articles, under the title "Our Critics, Right or Wrong," come forth with the passion, fury and force of Juvenal. There is much laying about with the whip. In all directions, before her flaying prose, go Elmer Davis, Irita van Doren, Joseph Wood Krutch (who sinned by liking

The Green Hat and praising Hugh Walpole's "readability"), Isabel Paterson, Herschel Brickell (his error was not only in recommending "meager, indistinguished novels," but in writing condescendingly of Gide's *The Counterfeiters*), Burton Rascoe (who, as one of the critical fraternity, praised fellow-critic Isabel Paterson's novel, *Never Ask the End,* as "superior to anything Virginia Woolf ever wrote").

The second article in which the by-line is transposed so that Mary McCarthy now appears first, concludes that "in ten years of literary criticism this small but potent group of anti-intellectuals have demonstrated that they prefer to festoon commonplace novels with the old clichés." Her girlish courage here is admirable; one must also mention the patience and courage of one of their targets, Joseph Wood Krutch who, while Mary McCarthy was lashing him and his colleagues in the pages of *The Nation,* was one of its Board of Editors.

In the third article, a new target was hit, the *Saturday Review* critics: Henry Seidel Canby, Christopher Morley, William Rose Benét, Amy Loveman and again, poor Elmer Davis. Canby is found to be culpable of praising Dorothy Parker's *Death and Taxes* while disliking *Sanctuary;* the lady critics of *Saturday Review,* Grace Frank and Gladys Graham, are guilty of "non-selective criticism." And the *New York Times* book reviewer, J. Donald Adams, fares no better. "His reviews are reports"; he is blamed for loving "romance, freedom, beauty; he hates dirty words, class warfare and dictatorships."

At this point in the barrage one of the whipped critics raised his bloody head to protest. *The Nation* printed a mild letter (considering) from Henry Seidel Canby deploring some "rather flagrant misstatements" made by "your young lady critics"; he goes on charitably to "deprecate such gross inaccuracy." His air is that of an indulgent father dealing with the misdeeds of bright but willful children.

The next target was the proletarian critics of *The New Masses.* They are treated pretty much as a group, not as individuals, and their errors, Marxist and stylistic, are held to be common to them all. They are accused of applauding any proletarian novel, no matter how inept, of being required to berate the bourgeoisie, and of regarding all faults of style as "minor." They must hew to the political party line; their errors are the result of their inferiority feelings on personal as well as aesthetic grounds. They are, in addition, afraid that they will mistakenly ignore writers needed by the Party, so *they* are praised as well.

The fourth article in the series appeared in mid-December of 1935. By this time another castigated critic stirred to protest. This issue contains a letter from furious Isador Schneider of *The New Masses,* who accuses "the ladies" of "giggling over" confusions which were, in reality, theirs. Neither this letter nor the one from Canby is entirely specific; both objectors content themselves with general expressions of dismay at the writers' temerity and harshness.

The final article took to task the book critics on daily newspapers. Here the obvious relation between art and merchandising is the central point. The conclusion, after John Chamberlain, Lewis Gannett and Harry Hansen have been raked over, is that "criticism is healthiest when it is farthest removed from publishers' advertising," in such journals as *The New Republic, The Yale Review, Virginia Quarterly, The Hound and Horn* and, of course, *The Nation.* This piece concludes with an unexpected twelve lines in which a few critics fit to be admired are actually noted. Listed are Rebecca West, Frances Newman, Louis Kronenberger, Robert Morse Lovett, Joseph Wood Krutch (who presumably recovered from his earlier slap on the wrist in time to be included here), and Edmund Wilson. These "have seemed, in varying degrees, perspicacious, but their faint catcalls have been drowned out by the bravos of the publishers' claque." However they do not go scot-free, with one notable exception: "None of these critics, with the exception of Mr. Wilson, has made any extended effort to relate what is valuable in modern literature to the body of literature in the past. Really vital criticism will probably not come until genuinely critical and independent minds can somehow communicate with the vast body of the reading public."

These five articles launched the intrepid young critic of critics into literary notice. The articles were notably well-written and daring; after the first one, because of the illness of Margaret Marshall (and despite the reassuring and stabilizing continuation of her name on the by-line), the articles were almost entirely the work of Mary McCarthy. They were followed in the next year by another article in *The Nation* called "Murder and Karl Marx," a consideration of detective fiction and politics, a subject of which Mary McCarthy had recently "made an intensive study." The result is a wittily stated conviction that in the last ten years (1926 to 1936) detective stories have become increasingly social-minded in the sense that they have "enlisted in the service of the status quo." Few of them "have taken up the cudgels of the downtrodden" (with the exception, she notes, of those by Carter Dixon). In these books she finds "stencils of villainy—the sinister Chinese, the surly day laborer, the oleaginous Jew." In them, too, proletarian characters are presumed guilty from the start, class lines are evident, and members of the upper classes are above suspicion, especially lovers, the aged and the clergy. Class lines have been drawn closely in this fiction; its authors "present a united front against any form of social innovation." Here "the young lady critic," demanding a true "class" awareness of the writers of detective fiction whom she claims have only the awareness of the upper class, is moving into a new area, sounding a new note for her; her class consciousness shows. She is not resting solely on her "bourgeois self" for a definition of what she regards as valuable in entertainment.

In the next year another "political" article appeared in the same magazine, this one called "Circus Politics in Washington State." Here the continuing development of Mary McCarthy's polemic style is evident. She attacks her subject bluntly, directly and with commanding force and indignation, and only her competence to deal with it at all, a competence that is to be called into question when she intrepidly launches into other fields, like art criticism, is in question. Indeed, the following month *The Nation* printed a letter entitled "Mary McCarthy and Her Critics" from one Selden C. Menefee deploring her lack of competence and information in the matter of Washington politics. It seems probable that Mary McCarthy's competence to do this piece stemmed from another of her "accidents": she "happened" to come from Seattle, she had been there recently during a big strike, and these facts were enough, at that time, to qualify her to write a piece on Washington State politics.

Mary McCarthy's career as journalist-critic was now well launched in New York. She decided in the spring of 1936 to divorce Harold Johnsrud.

Johnsrud, like Harald Petersen in *The Group,* was unemployed a good deal of the time. The theatre was still feeling the effects of the Depression, and when he did find acting or directing or writing jobs, they were often terminated abruptly: the plays closed, or the backer withdrew. Toward the end of their marriage, however, he had been working steadily—as the blind man in *Winterset.* They lived (as did Kay and Harald) in an expensive apartment, at her insistence, and had a part-time colored maid. They were usually in debt, often out of money. Once Mary McCarthy had to ask her family for money to pay for her appendix operation. She did not think of trying to get a full-time job (jobs were still scarce) and instead went on writing *Nation* reviews and editing and typing for Benjamin Stolberg, work that came to an end when Stolberg reached a personal literary impasse. At one point, to make money, she tried to write a detective story. Johnsrud wrote revue sketches, acted for the Theatre Union and in Archibald MacLeish's *Panic,* tried to sell stories to *The New Yorker* and to *Redbook,* and worked on stillborn projects for Jed Harris. An option on a play of his was bought by a producer, who at the same time took an option on Odets' *Awake and Sing.* Johnsrud's play was never done. Mary McCarthy no longer remembers whether, when he was working on a musical show, he was fired by a homosexual director or whether this incident, as described in *The Group,* was almost wholly "made up."

Like his prototype in *The Group,* Johnsrud had been unfaithful to his wife, although at the time Mary McCarthy was not aware of it. But in 1936, while he was out of town with a play, she met a young man named John Porter at a Webster Hall dance. Porter, a Williams graduate, charming and handsome rather in the manner of Fred MacMurray, was totally "unemployable." Their affair was well under way when Johnsrud returned from the road, and the breakup of their marriage became inevitable. In the late spring she decided upon a divorce. She notes in "My Confession" that separation from Johnsrud was followed by a week in June which she spent with Porter at Watermill, Long Island.

Then she took a train for Reno (an adventure on this trip is the source of the short story "The Man in the Brooks Brothers Shirt"), leaving both Porter and her husband of three years behind. When she returned to New York she was no longer interested in Porter, although he had been the ostensible cause of the divorce. She "moved into a one-room apartment—I had decided not to get married."

The breakup with Johnsrud and the trip to Reno is the subject of one story, "Cruel and Barbarous Treatment," which, it may be assumed, is an account, within the movable boundaries of fiction, of her feelings during this period. The heroine is "she," the prospective husband is called only the Young Man, and the husband appears in his lower-case, common-noun designation, except for his pronominal appearance when he becomes Him or His. The story concerns the husband and the Young Man only peripherally. It is a witty and stinging narrative about Her herself, and about her motives for divorce, which seem unattractive, egocentric and fanciful. She is actually not so much getting a divorce as enjoying enormously the *role* of the Young Divorcée. She sees her life in its most dramatic form, she is the star of the play, the "drama of the triangle" enthralls her; men have roles in the drama she is playing only so far as they support her vision of herself:

> She could not bear to hurt her husband. She impressed this on the Young Man, on her confidantes, and finally on her husband himself. The thought of Telling Him actually made her heart turn over in a sudden and sickening way, she said. This was true, and yet, she knew that being a potential divorcée was deeply pleasurable in somewhat the same way that being an engaged girl had been. In both cases, there was at first a subterranean courtship, whose significance it was necessary to conceal from outside observers.

The real-life actress that Mary McCarthy says she was (and it is only fair to note that she was the first to call attention to this trait in herself in *The Company She Keeps*) took the only action that seemed compatible with her feelings at the time. She was, apparently, bored with Johnsrud, among other things, disillusioned at his failures and weaknesses, incompatible with his moods; having been unfaithful to him, she felt she ought to leave him. She divorced him and then discovered she was equally bored with her fiancé. She writes (of Meg Sargent), "This interlude was at the same time festive and heartrending: her only dull moments were the evenings she spent alone with the Young Man." And again, in the autobiographical "Ghostly Father, I Confess," and in the guise of Meg Sargent again, we are given a glimpse of other causes for the terminus of her own marriage, indications of a growing instability, almost a hysteria, to which the conditions of the marriage had brought her. Again, for the fictional Aunt Clara, the reader might possibly substitute the real-life Aunt Margaret:

> The first time she got angry with her husband and heard a torrent of abuse pour from her own lips, she had listened to herself in astonishment, feeling that there was something familiar about the hysterical declamatory tone, something she could not quite place. It happened again and again... She had been married some time before she knew that she sounded exactly like Aunt Clara. Yet she could not stop, she was powerless to intervene when this alien personality would start on one of its tirades, or when it would weep or lie in bed in the morning, too wretched to get up. And when it began to have love affairs, to go up to strange hotel rooms, and try to avoid the floor clerk, she could only stand by, horrified, like a spectator at a play who, as the plot approaches its tragic crisis, longs to jump on the stage and clear up the misunderstanding, but who composes himself

> by saying that what is happening is not real, those people are only actors.
>
> "This isn't like you, Meg," her first husband would tell her, in that gentle voice of his, and she would collapse in his arms, sobbing, "I know I know, I know." She was inconsolable, but he could almost console her, since he shared her own incredulity and terror.

In this passage the reader has the eerie feeling of being spectator to a scene in which the author is looking at herself, as Meg, who is also watching herself, like the series of pictures within pictures on the old Dutch Cleanser cans. Meg (and the author) are horrified at themselves but clearly out of control, pushed to the near edge of breakdown by a relationship that no longer worked and which seemed almost to threaten their sanity.

As for Johnsrud, his subsequent history is full of pathos. His career in the theatre came to very little, he went on writing plays which were never produced, he formed an alliance with a young woman whom he was planning to marry when he died of lung burns in the Hotel Brevoort fire during the war. He is said to have escaped the fire and then gone back to try to rescue some manuscripts in his room. So, at the last, and by virtue of his marriage to Mary McCarthy and her use of him in *The Group,* he was to achieve the kind of immortality granted to near-portraits of real persons in widely read novels.

In 1936, now a divorcée and back in New York, Mary McCarthy was enjoying (at least for a while) the pleasures of living alone on Gay Street. "It was a period of intense happiness. . . . I moved into a one-room apartment on a crooked street in Greenwich Village and exulted in being poor and alone." She ate her meals alone at Shima's or the Jumble Shop on Eighth Street, or else cooked for herself in her apartment. She was for the first time her "owene woman, wel at ese." Occasionally she still saw Johnsrud, who was also living in the Village. Income was slim; at this time she received small, regular checks from her family. Her aloneness was perhaps intensified by the fact that the work she found to do she did at home. She had worked for a picturesque and unsuccessful art dealer, "Mr. Sheer," on and off during college and again during her marriage. Now she began to write brochures and descriptions of pictures for letters to his clients. (He was to be the subject of a memorable and ironic piece in *The Company She Keeps.*) Later in the year she went to work for him half-time at his gallery, while still free-lancing for *The Nation.* At this point she began to look seriously for a full-time job—for months without success.

This comparative isolation was not to last long. She began to make friends, partly through James Farrell and his wife. Another job appeared, this time with the publisher Covici-Friede, for whom she read manuscripts, at first at home, and then later at the office, where she learned what she now regards as the valuable techniques of a copy-editor, proofreader, etc. In her reading she came upon a story by Eudora Welty, and remembers that "reading her things for the first time was a pleasure." She wrote to her, "but nothing came of it."

In 1937, her life began to expand in many directions. She met Philip Rahv, a young Russian-born intellectual who had been an editor of *Partisan Review;* she remembers having seen him before at the Farrells' apartment. She gave him Russian manuscripts to read ("perhaps even some German ones") and their friendship grew into a lively, and what was to be, a much-gossiped-about affair. By summer a new free-lance job turned up, this time in Brooklyn, ghostwriting (with Ralph Craig) for H. V. Kaltenborn, his *Kaltenborn*

Edits the News. In the summer of 1937, she and Rahv moved into an apartment on Beekman Place they had borrowed from some wealthy friends, and in the fall of that year they took their own place on East End Avenue.

The quarterly *Partisan Review,* defunct after three years of troubled life, had begun in 1934 as a publication of the John Reed Club in New York. At its inception the board of editors was dominated by the Communists on it, and Rahv and William Phillips fought hard against the cultural Party line. In 1936, severely shaken by the Moscow trials, the magazine suspended publication until late in 1937, when it reappeared with its new "line"; it declared itself "independent of all party organizations and programs." Now strongly anti-Communist, it took on pro-Trotskyite coloration; when it reappeared, due to Rahv's influence, Mary McCarthy was on the staff, at first as a weekend worker, after her week-long job at Covici-Friede was over.

Of these days she later wrote: "I used to come down to the office on Saturdays . . . and listen to the men argue. . . . Once a month, late at night, after the dishes were done, I would write my 'Theatre Chronicle,' hoping not to sound bourgeois and give the Communists ammunition. . . . At that time (or should I say still?) nobody connected with the stage had ever heard of *Partisan Review.*"

Mary McCarthy claims that "the story that we on *Partisan Review* were Trotskyites" was an exaggeration. She explains that "the boys" were too "wary of political ties" to form others after they had all been through Communist Party experience. Only the backer was a political innocent—the backer and Mary McCarthy herself.

> My position was something like the backer's; that is, I was a source of uneasiness and potential embarrassment to the magazine which had accepted me, unwillingly, as an editor

> because I had a minute "name" and was the girl friend of one of the "boys," who had issued a ukase on my behalf. I was not a Marxist; I should have liked, rather, to be one, but I did not know the language, which seemed really like a foreign tongue.

The affair with Rahv increased the young writer's fame among the left-wing literati in New York, and was to give her some useful material when she came to write her *conte* on left-wing politics and thinking, *The Oasis.* Rahv is the original of the character Will Taub; he is, as well, the hero of all the gossip about her at this time. One interviewer reports that a "disgruntled listener" to the gossip complained to him: "Why is everybody always talking about her? Do you know I once knew more about Mary McCarthy and Philip Rahv than I knew about *myself?*" Rahv was reported to be furious at the author of *The Oasis;* it was rumored that he was threatening to sue her. Later she invited him to lunch early in the Fifties to discuss a new magazine she was thinking of starting. Her own attitude toward Rahv was never characterized by ill will (as so often happens with persons upon whom we knowingly inflict a hurt in some way). Indeed she seemed completely in the dark (the naïveté showing again) as to any reason he might have for resentment at his recognizable portrait, and genuinely surprised at his reaction. The 1956 edition of *Sights and Spectacles* (reviews which, in the main, had appeared in *Partisan Review)* is, in her apparently honest innocence of any wrong done, dedicated "To Philip and Nathalie Rahv." Rahv's wife, by the way, an architect, Nathalie Swan, was in Mary McCarthy's college class, but she left before the final year to go to the Bauhaus to finish her education and does not appear in *The Group.*

Another editor of *Partisan Review* at the time, Dwight

Macdonald, was destined for fictional recognition in *The Oasis,* and there are other people whom she knew in these years, either on *Partisan Review* or in the course of her contacts with the wider literary world of New York, who make partial, undignified, satiric appearances in the short novel. These years were fruitful ones for her, both in what she wrote and published in *Partisan Review* and as a source of fictional material ten years later.

Her assignment on *Partisan Review* was the theatre. She got it, as we have already noted, because it was known that she had recently been married to an actor. The editors worried about her bourgeois habits of mind. They "were always afraid I was going to do something that would disgrace *Partisan Review.*" She was given the status of editor, and had to be given something to do; the theatre, they reasoned, "was not worth bothering with . . . if I made mistakes, who cared?" Despite their lack of confidence she was "determined to make good." The column, surprisingly, turned out to be successful.

The magazine was Marxist, however undogmatic and non-conformist. Its editors attacked almost everything they dealt with—ideas in current acceptance, books, art, plays, films. "You could attack them in all honesty. Nobody else did it . . . we on *Partisan Review* were the only ones, as I recall, who were attacking right and left from an independent position." Conformist ideas were objects of their attack, and commercial success was "automatically suspected." Ambition, the pursuit of fame, were anathema, and she was later to explain this particular target in this way: "The American fear of failure . . . has its logical counterpart: the fear of success—of becoming one oneself or of admiring it in others. This was our (or my) besetting phobia, a product of the time, the place, and perhaps the person." Years later she discovered that *Come Back, Little Sheba* was "really quite good," but at the time, she admitted later, its commercial success had blinded her to its qualities.

Looking back over the years that "Theatre Chronicle" appeared in *Partisan Review,* Mary McCarthy is aware of the intellectual snobbery of the Thirties, and of the determined iconoclasm of the uncommitted Marxists. Her attitude was that "no one else would attack, so we did." Add this to her inborn love of wrecking the Establishment, her basic honesty, her strong, destructive, critical drive against everything she found shoddy or second-rate ("my judgments were mostly unfavorable"), the jargon of Marxist criticism ("my early reviews lisp the Marxist language"—a language she admits she acquired from the other editors by osmosis: "I was not one [a Marxist], but I took my line, as well as I could, from them")—and the quality of her theatre criticism can then be understood.

The violence, or perhaps, the strength, of Mary McCarthy's views about the theatre gained her an appreciative audience, although she says (somewhat disappointedly) that she never received a letter that disagreed with her opinions. A university professor said she was writing "the best theatre criticism he had read since Georg Brandes," a comment that embarrassed her because she had never heard of Brandes. Gore Vidal's admiration has already been noted. That she was hard on plays for one so young and so unknowledgeable in the specifics of the theatre was true. Her second husband, Edmund Wilson, told her: "You don't so much review a play as draw up a brief against it." At the time they were written her judgments struck many readers as overly severe, rigidly unyielding. To her hard young eye Maxwell Anderson, then at the height of his fame, was "essentially a popular playwright distinguished from his fellows only by his ambition." John Gielgud's *Hamlet,* a sell-out production and enormously popular, "was so decorated, so crammed with minutiae of gesture, pause, and movement that its general outline was imperceptible to an audience." Orson Welles, the wonder boy of the theatre in the Thirties, performed Brutus in *Julius Caesar* so that his interpretation "seemed to be based on the single theory that if you drop your voice two registers below the voices of the other actors you will give an impression of innocent saintliness." Of Clifford Odets, the white hope of the left-wing theatre, she wrote: "the narrowness of his invention, the monotony of his subject matter have anaesthetized him to a point where he must wade in blood and tears in order to feel that he is writing a play."

The lady-wrecker turned dramatic critic became a giant-killer of the first order, taking on even the most sacred of theatre persons. Of Ben Hecht's new play *To Quito and Back* (1937) she wrote: "The play, indeed, is a small, undignified moment of social and intellectual terror. The seesawings of the hero are a mere objectification of the nervousness of the author." Of William Saroyan (who comes off comparatively well and seems to have been able to move the stony young critic as few others did): "He is still able to look at the world with the eyes of a sensitive newsboy... the price is that the boundaries of this world are the boundaries of the newsboy's field of vision." She found Katharine Cornell's "devotion to her art... painfully sincere." Looking at herself from the vantage point of more than twenty years later, Mary McCarthy confesses that her earlier opinions are sometimes "insufferably patronizing... the voice of a young, earnest, cocksure, condescending cleverness." This is so, and it is interesting that her own ear is able to catch these overtones years later, but it is equally true that the judgments remain sound and time has in almost every case, borne them out. What she lacked at the time was not a keen eye for the pretentious or the fallacious or the theatrically unsound and limited, but the vacillating approach of contemporary criticism which would have softened the blows or so obscured them that the reading public would not have been aware they had fallen at all.

More remarkable than the harshness and sharpness of these reviews is the writing. Succinct and well put together, the sentences are so good that one forgets one is reading dramatic criticism, which is, all too often, scrappy, journalistic and lacking any discernible form. Of course Mary McCarthy was not working behind a deadline to produce these columns and, what seems to be equally productive of good theatrical writing, she "simply (did) not respond to the playwrights and popular actors that many other people find exciting." What is more, her approach to playwrights was a literary one. "I am troubled by the fact that most American plays are so badly written." Writing so well herself is part of the cause, and is to blame for much of her harshness; the rest lies in the iconoclastic tradition of the magazine itself, to which the wrecker-tradition in Mary McCarthy's blood readily corresponded. Her fierce and by now well-developed intelligence had simply, and early, lost interest in much that other critics accepted as entertaining. Only occasionally were her sympathies engaged by what she saw on the stage, and then she found herself somewhat at a loss to deal with the play. *Our Town* she liked, though she realized she ought not to like it. Later she said wryly: "I was almost afraid to praise it in the magazine, lest the boys conclude that I was starting to sell out." So she wrote with some measure of kindness about the contents of the play, its techniques and its theme, but felt obliged to salt her remarks with comments like "young love was never so baldly and tritely gauche as his [Wilder's] scene in the soda fountain suggests." She takes to task the philosophical contents of the third act: "The dead give some rather imprecise and inapposite definitions of the nature of the afterlife," unaware that to *require* precision of definition in a play of this sort, and *at this point* in the play, was excessively pedantic; it indicates her youth and eagerness not to "fall for" anything that provokes emotion in her. But more than of her years, the requirement she makes is significant of Mary McCarthy's quality of mind which demands *facts* as the bones of fiction, data for the flights of criticism and definitions from a stage. Without these (and they must, in addition, be well written) she becomes impatient with the literary product and irritated by its author. The result is often, as we have seen in these early judgments, widespread slaughter, a critical holocaust.

About the time these columns were beginning to appear periodically, Mary McCarthy published two articles in *The Nation* about her confrères on the aisle. To them she is as merciless as she was to the theatre people she was dealing with in *Partisan Review*. She reiterates a point she had been making in her "Theatre Chronicle"—that American critics know nothing about acting, rarely bother to deal with it at all, and when, in their ignorance, they do judge it, they make terrible mistakes. Just as she once found the book critics guilty of misleading the public by flabby, nondiscriminating reviewing, now she laid bare the "marrowless bones" of dramatic criticism which helped the actors not at all. "Dramatic criticism in America is at least purblind to acting."

The sinners of these articles—Richard Watts, Brooks Atkinson, Burns Mantle, John Mason Brown, and Richard Lockridge—have failed the public by misdirection and mis-instruction, she claimed. Thus, Atkinson identifies Katharine Cornell to his readers as "our queen of tragedy," while Mary McCarthy tells them that she "is considered by a great number of professionals no actress at all, but an ambitious, unimaginative, mediocre young woman whose fortune it is to own a face that is an exotic mask." Misguided critics, she says, have admired Miss Cornell inordinately while seriously underrating Ruth Gordon who "has for years been held to be one of our most expert actresses," presumably by the same great number of professionals. Lynn Fontanne's "talents are completely worn out (and this is no secret to the theatre)," although, clearly, the other critics were not aware of this truth.

In this article, again, Mary McCarthy finds fault with the critics who have made no attempt at a precise definition of the qualities in acting which seem to them good. Lack of precision, as well as ignorance, is their fault; they content themselves "with their frayed strings of vague but approbatory adjectives" and sometimes resort to the idiotic. So Katharine Cornell is praised by Robert Benchley for "improvement." Meaningless and imprecise words to describe acting are strewn about their reviews: "brilliant," "sincere," "moving." Critics faced with the necessity of saying *something* about the acting of a play like *Hamlet*—after all, "a critic can ignore the question of acting. But *Hamlet!*"—practice a kind of escapism. As she warms to her subject in the second of the two articles, Mary McCarthy slays by quotation, illustrating the contradictions contained in the critics' views of the same actor's performance. The whole fraternity of New York critics "are both frightened and lazy . . . [they] must go back to school to learn something of the techniques and standards of the profession which gives [them their] livelihood."

The answering barrage to this attack was not long in appearing although when it came it was, as the others had been, a kindly, mild rebuke. The young lady critic had been playing for real, but in the reply only blanks were fired. In his *Nation* letter Joseph Wood Krutch agreed that critics treat "plays more analytically than they do actors," and explained the reason. Undistinguished acting, common and widespread in the theatre, was hardly worth remarking upon, especially if there were interesting ideas in the play. Then too, seeing a part acted only once, by one actor, made it difficult for a critic to learn much about acting from comparison, etc. His reply is pleasant and humble: Now that we are seeing so many revivals "perhaps we shall learn more about acting." Gently he reminds Mary McCarthy that the daily paper's reports on plays are intended not for the actor or the student of acting but for the general reader.

* * *

In February 1938, having expressed her rarely given approval of Edmund Wilson in print two years before, Mary McCarthy gave him her private approval by marrying him. The marriage lasted more than twice as long as her first one, but it was stormy and a failure almost from the first day. It brought her closer to collapse and breakdown than at any time in her life.

Edmund Wilson was older than Mary—he was forty-three, she twenty-five—and this was his third marriage. He had graduated from Princeton near the end of World War I in the famous class that numbered F. Scott Fitzgerald among its members. Known as "Bunny" to Fitzgerald and his friends, Wilson was a round, amiable-looking man, of medium height, thinning reddish hair and brown eyes. He was absentminded, had a critical mind of the first rank, a strong scholarly bent, no aptitude for mechanical pursuits and an international reputation based on years as an editor (of *Vanity Fair* and *The New Republic*), many important reviews and studies in *The New Republic,* and a brilliant book of criticism, *Axel's Castle,* published in 1931.

Reportedly Edmund Wilson asked to meet Mary McCarthy because he very much admired her theatre criticism in *Partisan Review.* It was in the office of the magazine that they first met. A month after their marriage his book, *The Triple Thinkers,* was published. One review of this collection of critical essays is accompanied by a picture of the newlyweds. They stand looking at a book, presumably the new one, that they are both awkwardly holding, a quizzical look on Wilson's mature face, his almost-bald head and round face in curious contrast to his wife's youthful full bloom. She is the picture of the demure, apple-cheeked young girl, fresh out of convent school and delighted to find herself in the company of her elders. Her Irish features glow with pleasure, her grin is enormous.

Edmund Wilson, as Mary McCarthy recalls, was not so much quietly introspective as domineering in his views. Everything that happened came under his hand eventually and was shaped until it issued forth in what she calls "the authorized version." (But it is only just to point out here that this is perhaps a natural view of one party in a now-concluded marriage.) If Johnsrud had intrigued her partially because of his profession, to which she once thought she aspired, Wilson might have been, in some respects, an even more interesting prospect, a seemingly kind, fatherly figure, almost Olympian in his growing eminence in the literary world and formidable in his accomplishments. She admits freely that she didn't want to marry him, that she did so only at his insistence (she remembers that she said to him, girlishly, "I'm willing to live with you without marriage, but I don't want to marry you") and that from the first night, "with intervals," she was unhappy. But the fact is that she *did* marry him, and stayed with him far longer than one would have guessed, at least retrospectively, she would.

After her marriage, she gave up her job with Covici-Friede and went to live with Edmund Wilson in a house he had rented in Stamford, Connecticut. Almost at once she became pregnant, and the strain of this, together with the complete incompatibility of their personalities, brought her perilously close to the edge of nervous collapse. Late in that spring, after much serious disagreement and while they were in the process of moving in Stamford "from the place on the river which was so beautiful" to another house, Mary McCarthy was admitted to Payne Whitney Clinic. The version of this story in Chapter Thirteen of *The Group* is now well known. Kay is admitted to Payne Whitney with a black eye and bruises, given her by her husband, Harald, who had been drinking. She is in a somewhat hysterical state, although not confused or demented, and she has landed in Payne Whitney as the result of a misunderstanding. Both she and Harald supposed, at the outset, that she was going to the regular New York Hospital (*not* to the psychiatric wing) to rest for a few days; the doctor had suggested Harkness Pavilion, but Kay, with her characteristic obstinacy, had insisted on New York Hospital because she preferred the decor and "all her friends" went there to have babies. In the clinic, when Harald has left her with her suitcase, she discovers that she is in a mental hospital. They want to take away her belt and wedding ring; the doctor, being a psychiatrist, assumes that her black eye is self-inflicted. Harald, who has gone off on a drinking bout, eventually turns up and admits to the doctor that he has beaten her. But because she has Blue Cross (a fact unearthed by Harald's mistress, Norine), she agrees to stay on for a "cooling off period" between her and Harald rather than pay for a hotel room. She is moved to a convalescent floor by the psychiatrist; this satisfies her vanity. It is typical of Kay that she would not mind being in an insane asylum—and indeed would rather enjoy it, as a sort of privileged tourist—so long as everyone there recognized that she was "different"—*i.e.*, sane.

How close these events in *The Group* are to Mary McCarthy's own life it is difficult at this distance to ascertain. As a former Covici-Friede employee, she did have Blue Cross. As for the rest, she is perhaps no longer sure where fiction began, "for actually when you write about something you get mixed up afterwards about which version is true." Kay is close to Mary McCarthy in many ways, and Harald, to whom Kay is married, is, it would seem, a conglomerate figure. After her discharge from Payne Whitney, Mary McCarthy went back to the house at Shippan Point and to her marriage to Edmund Wilson.

Amazingly enough, during the upsetting months of her pregnancy, she went on doing her "Theatre Chronicle," and she was working in a new literary form as well. Edmund Wilson had decided that his wife ought to write fiction. She recalls: "We'd been married about a week, and he said, 'I think you've got a talent for writing short stories.' So he put me off in the one free room at Stamford with a typewriter and shut the door. I wrote 'Cruel and Barbarous Treatment' straight off, without blotting a line."

The charm of this anecdote lies partly in its familiarity. Edmund Wilson's behavior toward his wife (someone has said: "He treated her like a schoolgirl") is reminiscent of the story of Henry-Gautier Villars, called Willy by his wife, Colette. Willy, described by Glenway Wescott as "a bad, clever, corpulent, somewhat crazy man," fifteen years older than the twenty-year-old Colette, was a hack writer by profession. At his suggestion, she became his ghostwriter. Wescott's account of the start of *her* career is that "he would lock her in her room for four-hour stretches while she inked up a certain number of pages . . . thus in servitude, page by page, she became a professional writer."

Without the locked-door detail and the illegal use of her material under his own name, these conditions were close to Mary McCarthy's introduction to the writing of fiction. She has told the story another way: "He said, 'I think you have a talent for writing fiction.' He didn't literally lock the door, but he said, 'Stay in there,' and I did. I just sat down, and it just came."

"It" was *The Company She Keeps,* published in 1942, the same year that Edmund Wilson's own novel appeared. *Memoirs of Hecate County,* his second sortie into the field of fiction, is still his "favorite among my books—I have never understood why the people who interest themselves in my work never pay any attention to it." Mary McCarthy, up to this time, had had no ambition to be a novelist; after this, rightly or not, she was one. "I suppose," she told Elisabeth Niebuhr in *The Paris Review,* twenty years later, "I consider myself a novelist."

III *Rare Birds of New York*

"I'm not sure any of my books are novels. Maybe none of them are. Something happens in my writing—I don't mean it to—a sort of distortion, a sort of writing on the bias, seeing things with a sort of swerve and sweep."

—*Paris Review,* "Writers at Work," 1961.

A YEAR after her marriage to Edmund Wilson, Mary McCarthy's only child, Reuel Kimball Wilson, was born on Christmas Day, 1938. Living variously in Stamford, Wellfleet, Chicago (while Wilson taught at the University), Truro and New York, she continued to contribute her "Theatre Chronicle" to *Partisan Review,* and began, at Wilson's suggestion, to write a series of short stories which appeared first in *Southern Review, Partisan Review* and *Harper's Bazaar.* In 1942, living in Wellfleet in a house which they bought and remodeled (and in which Wilson still lives), with Wilson and her young son and usually spending the winter and spring in New York, she gathered the scattered stories together into a volume called *The Company She Keeps.*

The first edition, which Simon and Schuster published in 1942, contained a foreword which later editions eliminated. It concludes with this paragraph:

> It is not only scenes and persons but points of view that are revisited—the intimate "she," the affectionate, diminutive "you," the thin, abstract, autobiographical "I." If the reader is moved to ask: "Can all this be the same person?" why, that is the question that both the heroine and the author are up against. For the search is not conclusive; there is no deciding which of these personalities is the "real" one; the home address of the self, like that of the soul, is not to be found in the book.

It is reasonable to assume that Mary McCarthy removed the foreword from the reissue, the Harcourt, Brace edition, because she was no longer concerned, eighteen years later, that the reader would misconstrue her intent, however thin and abstract, or miss the unity of person disguised under the change of narrative person from story to story. This first book of fiction contains six stories which are tied together by two means: a pronominal switch, and by the use of the quest theme in almost a modern picaresque form, the search for self, which is made more poignant by the inability of the narrator to assume (or find) a single person to be. "It is a case of lost identity. The author and the reader together accompany the heroine back over her life's identity."

The theme of these stories, in varying degrees of intensity, is the pursuit by a disturbed girl of her true identity, a painful, excoriating search that proceeds single-mindedly with only peripheral reference to people she meets on the way. She is driven by a need to know, to become one person, one pronoun. This need becomes intensified during the quest, and at the last becomes a need for *amour-propre,* so consuming that it caused her "to snatch blindly at the love of others, hoping to love herself through them." During the search the heroine recognizes her own ambiguous relationship to society, a recognition that carries with it a love of acting, "being" someone else, together with an affection for the social strays she encounters along the edges of New York life. The search for a lost self, a divided personality reaching out for alliances to make it whole, brings into the scope of these stories a number of fascinating oddities.

The five stories assume full meaning only in the sixth, "Ghostly Father, I Confess." Here, terrible (and often funny) humiliations in one love and one bed after another culminate. Here the earlier, sometimes shocking encounters are melted down to a general truth. Love, men and marriage are reduced to the lowest denominator of frankness and common sense, a position they are to maintain throughout all of Mary McCarthy's subsequent work. But, contrary to a widely held view—most recently advanced by John Aldridge in his long chapter, "Mary McCarthy: Princess Among the Trolls," in *Time to Murder and Create*—this denigratory process does not, as Aldridge insists, elevate the female. His claim that

> ...it is perfectly in keeping with the logic of her moral hypocrisy that at the end Margaret's snobbishness is fully and now quite guiltlessly reaffirmed. She has paid the price for feeling superior; she has suffered and sacrificed for it; and so is now free to relax and enjoy it. At the end she is indeed "myn owene woman, wel at ese."

is, I think, a misinterpretation, the result of mistaking the part, the single story, for the whole, the novel. By a reverse process the female in Mary McCarthy is not elevated to princess, but instead fragmented, her personality shattered, by her contact with the male. In no other place is this as clear as in "Ghostly Father, I Confess," when Meg Sargent's arrogance and egoism (always, I think, offered ironically) are brought low, to the hysteria and confusion of the psychiatrist's couch.

"Cruel and Barbarous Treatment" is the first story, and

we have already noticed that it contains some interesting autobiographical revelations about the state of its author's mind and emotions during and just after the termination of her first marriage. The heroine, "she," is a self-dramatizing young woman, and her emotional tangles are accompanied by postures which, often, she enjoys more than she suffers. Indeed, whatever suffering might have been involved in a love affair, a break with her husband, and a departure for Reno, is buried under the frank delight she feels *playing* the role. "She had an intense, childlike curiosity as to How Her Husband Would Take It, a curiosity she disguised for decency's sake as justifiable apprehension." And later: "Terrified, she wondered whether she had not already prolonged the drama beyond its natural limits, whether the confession in the restaurant and the absolution in the Park had not rounded off the artistic whole, whether the sequel of divorce and remarriage would not, in fact, constitute an anticlimax." In her emotional life the play's the thing, and she moves from role to role, speaking her lines, and thinking in terms of the recognized clichés of dramatic marital situations.

An interesting technical device in this story is the use of capital letters to set apart the clichés of social intercourse which are the vocal manifestations of how people then thought. So we come upon Public Appearances, Woman with a Secret, The Situation Was Impossible, Things Couldn't Go On This Way Any Longer, and so on. The device reminds the reader that the *character,* not the *novelist,* is thinking, at least at the moments that the clichés are used to formulate thought. That we suspect, outside of the novel, that occasionally it is also the novelist's *view* does not detract from the effectiveness of the technique. For the moment we are thinking as Meg Sargent is thinking, or better, as the world around her shaped her way of thought. The technique

MARY McCARTHY, 1949. *Courtesy of Ralph Ellison*

Sylvia Salmi, Courtesy of Mary McCarthy

WITH EDMUND WILSON AT WELLFLEET, CAPE COD, 1941–42

WITH REUEL IN RED BANK, 1939.

Courtesy of Mary McCarthy

E
F P
T O Z
L P E D
C F D
C Z P
P Z D

ATE 1930s.

ourtesy of Mary McCarthy

CIRCA 1952–53.

Kevin O'Flaherty McCarthy, Courtesy of Mary McCarthy

Courtesy of Mary McCarthy

WITH BOWDEN BROADWATER, TRUESDALE BEACH, WESTPORT HARBOR.

REUEL AT HOME IN PORTSMOUTH, NEWPORT, 1952–53.

Courtesy of Mary McCarthy

Kevin O'Flaherty McCarthy, Courtesy of Mary McCarthy

AT WELLFLEET, CAPE COD, SUMMER, 1954.

provides us as well with certain, exact, historical data for the story, the data of verbal currency, and thus, subtly, of the thought of the time. Capitalized words become period indicators, speech clichés common to the late Thirties. They are vocal, conversational markers for an era in That Kind of Thought. Much later, in *The Group,* Mary McCarthy is to try another kind of voice technique, another attempt to break through the tired confines of straight third-person narrative. This first experiment, slight as it is, is interesting and successful. It is a sign that she felt the need to find a means for other-voice projection, a tonal differentiation among the possibilities offered by author, heroine, and other necessary speakers in her fiction, without the directive use always of "said."

"Cruel and Barbarous Treatment" is about the dramatic roles that love makes possible to a woman, the performance-nature of her behavior in relation to men. The heroine acts under the conviction that her life and emotions take on meaning only as they are presented to the outer world, and as that outer world would approve of them. (" 'I couldn't really love a man,' she murmured to herself once, 'if everybody didn't think he was wonderful.' ") Somewhat like Madame Bovary, who found near the end of her affair with Leon that "adultery could be as banal as marriage," she realizes that "the virtue of marriage as an institution lay in its public character. Private cohabitation, long continued, was, she concluded, a bore." And while she concedes the difficulties of her new role as Divorcée we leave her at the end boarding a train, imbued with a sense of her new importance, and determined to deal appropriately with the other travelers who might talk to her in the club car.

"Rogue's Gallery," the second story, is written in the form of memoirs, as if the heroine, now become "I," had recorded what she remembered of a curious encounter. Mary McCarthy-I, the narrator, confesses to an affection for Mr. Sheer, the rogue who owns a specious "gallery dealing in objects of art." Mr. Sheer is not unrelated to the heroine of "Cruel and Barbarous Treatment." As it was to her, "masquerade was life to Mr. Sheer. He could not bear to succeed in his own personality, any more than an unattractive woman could bear to be loved for herself." He is, like the heroine of the first story, enjoying his role and relishing life only when it is played by someone other than his real self.

Like Martha in a later novel, *A Charmed Life,* Mary McCarthy has a distinct taste for frauds, which again suggests the affections of the picaresque novelist. This fondness is allied to her dislike, expressed in her college essay on Harington and her theatre criticism, of ambition out of proportion to talent, or of success as an end in itself. Success becomes an oddly exotic flower that grows only in fake, pretentious, fraudulent gardens. In *A Charmed Life* the vicomte's "rich air of fraudulence" is described with affection; again, in a later collection of stories, *Cast a Cold Eye,* Mr. Sciarappa, "The Cicerone," appears as another lovingly drawn fraud. In this sense, the currents of the eighteenth-century novel run strong in Mary McCarthy. We have seen her use of the quest theme translated into modern terms of a search for self; in "Rogue's Gallery" we meet a second eighteenth-century fictional taste of hers, a fondness for picaresque subjects, brought to a typically modern turn. The roguish Mr. Sheer is caught sight of in a series of shady events that bring him to the bottom of his financial resources and to the end of his fancy evasions and promises. At the end of the story he is prosperous, and like the heroine, he finds his success incredible. Because he cannot understand why fate has so suddenly turned on him, he is uneasy. Now that he has reached "the apogee of his career" he is puzzled by his unhappiness. Personally elusive and slippery by nature, he is made restive by success and bored by legitimate enterprises. He is rejuvenated at the last only by the vitiating prospect of a dangerous operation during which he may die. "And for the first time in many weeks he giggled irrepressibly." Mr. Sheer, like his creator, distrusts success and sees a certain virtue in lack of popularity and recognition. It is the old, comfortable consolation of the bohemian. The heroine, like the author, is still a bohemian girl, as she is to characterize herself in the next story.

This is the most famous, most notorious of all her stories. "The Man in the Brooks Brothers Shirt" had appeared earlier in *Partisan Review,* and caused Mary McCarthy to be widely discussed in New York literary circles as well as much talked about in cultivated academic circles throughout the country. For a long time, and until publication of *The Group,* it is fair to say that only a coterie knew much about her work. The single exception was "The Man"; it was read, or at least known and talked about, for the same reasons that *The Group* was to be. It was responsible for her early reputation as a "racy" or "sexy" writer.

"The Man" is another journey story, translated into Pullman car terms; to note its surface resemblance to something like an episode in *Joseph Andrews* or *Tom Jones* is not too farfetched. The heroine is halfway through a cross-continental journey west to Portland to tell her aunt she is about to be remarried. The train is passing through Nebraska when, in the club car, Meg (the She and I now for the first time given a proper-noun name) begins a conversation with a traveling salesman "in steel," Bill Breen. They go to his compartment ("Don't worry. . . . It'll be perfectly proper. I promise to leave the door open"), drink a great deal, and exchange details of their lives. The salesman comes from Cleveland, lives in a fourteen-room house with his two small sons and his wife Leonie, who "loves her house and children. Of course, she was interested in culture, too, particularly the theatre, and there were always a lot of young men hanging about her; but then she was a Vassar girl, and you had to expect a woman to have different interests from a man." She is, in addition, a Book-of-the-Month-Club member. Breen buys his haberdashery at Brooks Brothers, all "except ties and shoes." In her turn, Meg tells him of her job on *The Liberal,* conscious that she is now, in the compartment, playing a new part. In the club car she has been the great lady, now to the traveling salesman she is metamorphosed into the Bohemian Girl. She becomes in her own eyes what she thinks she is to his. Her disillusion with the New York literary world falls away:

> What she got from his view of her was a feeling of uniqueness and identity, a feeling that she had once had when, at twenty, she had come to New York and had her first article accepted by a liberal weekly, but which had slowly been rubbed away by four years of being on the inside of the world that had looked magic from Portland, Oregon.

They talk politics, they talk about their marriages. His undeviating literary opinions remind her of a cousin "who was like that about the theatre," and she remembers how her aunt used to complain, saying, "It's no use asking cousin Florence whether the show at the stock company is any good this week; cousin Florence had never seen a bad play." There was almost no fiction to this memory which is taken whole, another evidence of her use of experience to shore up a character. In *Memories* she tells us that:

> . . . to Aunt Eva there were no distinctions. Every play she saw she pronounced "very enjoyable." And of the actors: "They took their parts well." We used to laugh at her and

> try to get her to acknowledge that the play was better some weeks than others. But Aunt Eva would not cross that Rubicon; she smelled a rat. To her, all the plays and players were equal, and equally, blandly good.

Mr. Breen is given Aunt Eva's bourgeois pursuit of culture without the intelligence to do anything with it.

Meg ends the remembered part of the drunken evening by quoting her favorite line from Chaucer's *Troilus and Creseyde:* "I am myn owene woman, wel at ese." The wishful thinking, the irony and the furious untruth of this becomes apparent to her when she awakens next morning in his compartment and his bed, with him naked beside her. At this point, and once her moral horror at "this sin" is over, Meg realizes (as do many Mary McCarthy heroines in other sexual situations) the purely ludicrous elements in her situation, "the comic nature" of the loss of a garter, the safety pin she discovers in her underwear, her need to throw up when the salesman awakens and tells her he loves her. The details of the night before, full of bribed porters and vague recollections of the perverse violences that were preliminary and necessary to the act itself, at first disgust, then amuse her: "If the seduction . . . could be reduced to its lowest common denominator, could be seen in farcical terms, she could accept and even, wryly, enjoy it. The world of farce was a sort of moral underworld, a cheerful, well-lit hell where a Fall was only a prat-fall after all." In her second novel, Mary McCarthy generalizes about the sexual prowess of businessmen: of Joe Lockwood in *The Oasis* she says: "like many virile business leaders, he was sexually recessive," and this generalization may cast some retroactive light on Breen.

Now the story itself falls away into cleanup details. At his insistence Meg takes a bath, they breakfast (a "ceremonial feast" such as all primitive peoples indulge in after "a cataclysmic experience"), he confesses his disappointment with his life and she, curiously, begins to like and understand this businessman, the sort of person who, in all her previous experience, had seemed so gross and stereotyped.

Charles Eisinger in his book on *The Fiction of the Forties* thought that the "clash of two cultures," the Bohemian-liberal-intellectual and the business-bourgeois, dated this story, that it is now merely "redolent of the thirties"—and no longer true. Another critic, Mason Wade, denied the existence of the conflict in these terms by claiming that Meg was "a pseudo-intellectual woman." Neither, it seems to me, takes sufficient note of the feminine element at this point in the story which is not symbolic or typic but psychologically accurate.

> "I love you," she said suddenly. "I didn't before, but now I do."
> The man glanced sharply at her.
> "Then you won't get off the train?"
> "Oh, yes," she said, for now at last she could be truthful with him. "I'll certainly get off. One reason I love you, I suppose, is because I *am* getting off."
> His eyes met hers in perfect comprehension.
> "And one reason I'm going to let you do it," he said, "is because you love me."
> She lowered her eyes, astonished, once more, at his shrewdness.

She gets off the train, knowing now that there is no point to her trip home—"she was never going to marry the young man back in New York." Their last meeting and then their parting are anticlimatic horrors. He falls back into the Reactionary-Big Businessman stereotype, and finally is transformed into the expected, cliché-spouting fool. The brief, funny, touching encounter is over. Meg has made another try at a Relationship and failed again.

Mr. Breen is, in some ways, more masculine, more direct, than the usual Mary McCarthy males, truncated, wispy, weird underdog spirits against which her fictional females pose themselves to be seen and understood by the reader. Their male inadequacies, their little oddities, are recessive traits necessary for the definition of the dominant traits of her feminine characters. She knows this herself, of course—it is no discovery of mine—and so she takes much of the starch out of the discovery. As the reader becomes aware that her world is a muliebrity served and heightened by diluted masculinity, he is forced to confess that *she* was aware of it first, indeed, Meg pointed it out to him somewhere back there:

> . . . Somehow each of them was handicapped for American life and therefore humble in love. And was she, too, disqualified, did she really belong to this fraternity of cripples, or was she not a sound and normal woman who had been spending her life in self-imposed exile, a princess among the trolls?

Pflaumen, the "Genial Host" of the next story, is related to Mr. Sheer in Mary McCarthy's continuing study of society's trolls. Like Sheer he is an outcast, a nonentity in himself; like Meg, he is searching for an identity, trying to establish it by the use of his dinner guests. These carefully selected persons are to him not so much real as allegorical, figures whom he has creatively matched and set down beside each other in his own meaningful microcosm. He entertains in order to make serious inroads into the lives of his friends, to become inextricable parts of them, to form alliances that will define *his* personality for him. Mr. Sheer lives on the illusions of danger, Mr. Pflaumen creates a vision of himself by means of his visitors. Later, in *Cast a Cold Eye,* these become allied to the ephemeral Francis Cleary, the "Friend of the Family," and to the vicomte of *A Charmed Life,* all memorable, compassionately conceived social orphans, themselves closely related, one would guess, to the actress in their creator as much as representative of the company she kept.

Meg's final encounter, except for the session with the weak-headed psychiatrist in the last story of the cycle, is with Jim Barnett, the Yale Man of "Portrait of the Intellectual as a Yale Man." More than the other characters in the book, Jim is close (in appearance at least) to a real person, the critic and editor John Chamberlain, and yet he is less an exact representation than many of her other characters. Mary McCarthy contends, with perfect sincerity, that she used only John Chamberlain's good looks "and a few features of his career," but even Chamberlain himself has on occasion made note, almost fondly, of the identification. Prefacing Chamberlain's review of *The Group,* the *National Review* editor introduces the reviewer as the man that Mary McCarthy was "having fun with" in her story. Chamberlain in his own summary study of Mary McCarthy in a volume called *The Creative Present* admits he ought to be galled by the portrait of himself but is not: "I have never been able to see myself in Jim Barnett's shoes." Mary McCarthy reiterates the lack of identification and adds that in this story *she* is not Meg. "It was while I was doing the one about the Yale man that I decided to put the heroine of the earlier stories in that story too. The story of the Yale man is not a bit autobiographical. . . ." The use of a few surface characteristics and a few generalizations in the progress of a career that may well be typical of Yale men who come to New York and go into journalism are the sort of thing she does customarily in the creation of character. Her constructions are bits and snatches of autobiography, remembered details, half of one person, a piece of another. The rest in this case, clearly, is fiction.

If the subject of the earlier stories was the fragmented, individual psyche of I-You-She-Meg-Mary, here it is an objective, social observation: that it is easy for the idealistic, attractive young intellectual to be seduced by success if he abandons his liberalism (not very sturdy to start with) and joins forces with the Establishment. Jim represents, far more than a real person, the onset of Mary McCarthy's generalized study of the intellectual in society, suggested less distinctly in the "Brooks Brothers" story by Meg's encounter with Mr. Breen. Jim is no Breen to the heroine, not an antagonist but instead, initially, a kindred spirit. The story asserts the author's doubts about the staying power and integrity of the intellectual. Her career-long depiction of the type is to continue through the satire of *The Groves of Academe* and into her study of the intellectually defective graduates of *The Group* who, because of their education, might be expected, as part of the commonly held cliché, to be intellectuals or to make some pretenses themselves in this direction. Jim is the hero of this story, Meg merely a camera eye, a recording ear for his progress or lack of it, a listener to his self-doubts. Most of the time Jim is alone with the reader, without even the presence of Meg's eye, and here for the first time in this volume the knowing author tells the story straight without the intervention of Meg's sensibility. From the intellectual point of view Jim represents those young men who played with the radical issues of the Thirties, the kind of man whose convictions were ephemeral, the proper ones at the time, growing out of "a deficiency of imagination. Jim did not believe that Trotsky could have plotted to murder Stalin or to give the Ukraine to Hitler, because he could not imagine himself or anybody he knew behaving in such a melodramatic and improbable manner." He brings to his mature life and developing thinking all the "intelligent mediocrity of the Yale man."

Here the Vassar girl (who later will make the same kind of summary for Vassar's product in general) speaks:

> But at Yale a certain intellectual prodigality had been cultivated in the students; it was bad taste to admire anything too wholeheartedly. They thought "bad taste" but they meant "dangerous," for the prodigality was merely an end product of asceticism: you must not give in to your appetites, physical or spiritual; if you did, God knows where it would land you, in paganism, Romanism, idolatry, or the gutter. Like all good Yale men, Jim feared systems as his great-grandfather had feared the devil, the saloon, and the pope.

Meg has one brief, sexual encounter with clean-cut, Yale-man-intellectual, married Jim; their business relationship at the *Liberal* office becomes his excuse for not renewing the event. Sternly faithful to her Trotskyite views, Meg is demoted because of the Stalinist convictions of the literary editor and, faced with the prospect of Meg's being fired, Jim walks out as well, presumably to write a book he has been thinking about. His intentions come to nothing, he is hired by a prestigious *Life*-like picture magazine called *Destiny,* which gradually turns him into a seedy, alcoholic, "professionally bewildered" editor-writer, still somewhat liberal. His Yale-formed mind, good, naïve and honest as we saw it in the earlier part of the story, weakens under success. Only when he occasionally comes upon Meg at parties is he aware of the schism between them, and in himself. He keeps her from getting a job on *Destiny,* he tells himself he does not envy her unhappy, poverty-stricken, and free state of failure, and yet he feels a curious regret, a sense that he has lost his own freedom. "He had never been free, but until he had tried to love the girl, he had not known he was bound . . . she had showed him the cage of his own nature. He had accommodated himself to it, but he could never forgive her.

Through her he had lost his primeval innocence, and he would hate her forever as Adam hates Eve."

What is this story *about?* Primarily, the tension in the lives of young, educated, privileged liberals of the Thirties between integrity of conviction (which, in Mary McCarthy's eyes sometimes accompanies poverty and failure) and the seductiveness of success which requires of the intellectual an abandonment of the "true" path. When Meg claims in this story that "I am not even political," and then explains her defense of Trotsky as "he's the most romantic man in modern times," she is being both pleasantly social to Jim and completely feminine in her desire to strike out at the smugness of the *Liberal*'s editors. What she is implying, however, is that her convictions are *ethical,* not narrowly political, and that she is defending the integrity and courage of the man who did not "scramble" for position, either morally, socially, or politically, just as, in action, she herself does not scramble for success, and Jim, poor weak Yale man, does.

There is an old-fashioned air about this story because the terms under which Jim and Meg are judged (or judge themselves) are so absolute, so clearly defined. The intellectual puritan in Mary McCarthy, whom we will meet again and again, seems to speak out clearly—and the equation of success with dishonesty, rigid as it is, becomes formularized for the first time here. Even the phraseology is old-fashioned: "He took her twice" takes one back to the novels of Victorian tradition. Defection from conviction is the major sin, and Jim suffers accordingly. He loses his "pink cheeks and sparkling brown eyes," and with the loss of his looks and sobriety, of his "primal innocence," he takes his place in the little platoon of McCarthy heroes, fibreless, less-than-adequate accommodaters to the status quo. It might be noted here that many of the liberals in her work and the male hero begin to have a number of characteristics in common: their spinelessness, their lack of honesty, their easy fall from strength and virtue.

The culminative story, "Ghostly Father, I Confess," as we have said, serves retrogressively to illumine the other five. Here the method and the content of the stories are justified. The unnamed heroine of "Cruel and Barbarous Treatment" has no past; here she is provided with one, and brings her terrible history into her own consciousness and ours, not so much in what she says to her "confessor," the psychiatrist, but in what she allows her own mind to deal with silently during the session. A *New York Times* reviewer of this book suggested that what was wrong with Meg was that "her perspective was distorted" and that her temperament was "diseased and self-destroying." While it might somehow be possible to see this final story as revelatory of mental illness it is not the answer that Mary McCarthy gives in the story. During the hour that Meg lies on the couch, we are permitted to watch a woman whose childhood has scarred her ruinously, whose intelligence has failed at this time to save her, whose maturity is finally being reached only at the cost of her permanent abandonment of any hope of a unified personality. What is wrong with her seems not so much to be mental distortion or disease but a realistic if painfully achieved maturity, perhaps true to some extent of all human beings confronted with breakdown who end by accepting a "cure" which is less than the whole self.

Early in the confession Meg tells of a dream, of when she was seventeen and went to an outing cabin owned by her college. Then, breaking off, she launches into an ingenious literary attack on the psychiatrist, Dr. James. Clearly, at this moment, Meg is trying to substitute her recognized, clever, literary self for the ones she knows lie next to it. She is avoiding self-conviction in this way; eventually she must come to that. Completely unstrung, she cries on the couch even while she is capable of foreseeing and predicting Dr. James' questions and conclusions. Meg dissects herself (" 'Ah,' she thought, 'thank God for the mind, the chart, the compass' ") and finds only confusion (" 'You have got everything upside down,' her husband told her"), nameless grief, revolt against the "ugly cartoon of middle-class life," and "the middle-class tragedy" of her orphaned childhood. She goes over her own unsavory immediate past—the affairs, the wreck of her marriage—she brings her "skeptical prosaic intelligence" to bear upon the moral and psychical crises of her life, and as the psychiatrist talks she reviews her own state of near-hysteria. She realizes that she began to collapse soon after her first marriage and that only temporarily had she been reprieved by divorce. Again and again, in other "relationships" the crying jags recur, the sense of being trapped returns in her second marriage. Always she has escaped, moved on, but now, brought finally to the couch, and under the psychiatrist's prodding, she acknowledges that she is now conquered, "overrun by barbarian tribes," who may be the men she has known. The psychiatrist ends the hour by assuring her she can get back her "rights" of decision, either to leave her husband or be reconciled to him, by the use of her two "weapons," her mind and her beauty. Only after she has left his office, preening herself on his reference to her beauty, wondering if he. . . ? does she recall the end of her dream, in which three dun-colored heavy-featured tall young men, "like the pictures of Nazi prisoners," accompanied by two low-class girls, invade the outing cabin and a party begins. She flirts with one of the men, who then metamorphoses into a handsome, Byronic, sensitive fellow (suddenly wholly acceptable). He kisses her, she keeps her eyes closed against his beastliness, and the extremity to which she has been brought sweeps over her:

"it was some failure in self-love that obliged her to snatch blindly at the love of others, hoping to love herself through them. . . ." Finally she acknowledges the truth about herself, that for her the failures of blind flesh can only be rescued by the perception of the spirit, that she can survive only if she does not yearn fruitlessly for total assimilation of her undigestible experience, for perfect unity of her fragmented self. The story ends on a classical note. Like the hero of *The Groves of Academe,* who brings the last scene in that novel to a close by quoting a famous line from a Ciceronian oration, Meg quotes Catullus. An unbeliever, she prays for her survival on these new terms of disunity: *"O di, reddite me hoc pro pietate mea* [O gods, render this to me in return for my devotion]."

In this highly introspective and touching story Mary McCarthy has thrown all autobiographical caution to the winds. Her honesty is absolute and painful. The variety of self that is Meg Sargent is irrevocably tied to her self-knowledge. She reveals her deep, if partial, resentment of men, she displays her tendency to sexual puritanism ("that dirty fornication in the hotel room"), she does continuous penance for the wayward acts of her young life that seem to have come about out of a need for freedom, like a trapped animal that hurts itself terribly in its efforts to escape a trap, because of her "festering conscience." She realizes the true nature of the self is to be unknown, unapproachable, and chameleonlike, and that one of the values of the search for self lies in the meanders of incidental, colorful social encounters, so that in the process of running Meg to ground we, as well as she, end by discovering Mr. Sheer, Pflaumen, Jim Barnett, and the long-suffering, wrong-headed Dr. James.

Critics have both admired and been hard on this book,

divided as to its value. Malcolm Cowley said the book was not likable; John Chamberlain saw it as "a judgment on the playgirl as a romantic revolutionary," while Charles Eisinger thought quite the opposite, that "nothing was on trial, not middle-class society, not the liberated intellectual personality, not even womanhood itself." Chamberlain thought the book possessed "a scientific, unflagging curiosity about sex," like Kinsey's, he adds, and in addition "a pitiless insistence on seeing everything." Mary McCarthy's "admirable intelligence" is "without imaginative depth or emotional profundity," he claims; he ends by accusing her of the same charge she brought against Barnett: "deficiency of imagination."

Some critics were deceived by the purposeful disjointedness of the method of dealing with the subject into thinking that the book resulted in "discontinuity and lack of cumulative effect." Some agreed that the tone of the book was "malicious," or "spiteful"; a few found it witty, others just "sharp," and "lacking in charity." Perhaps the unkindest review of all (as it turned out, the one least characterized by acumen) came from Clifton Fadiman, then the book reviewer for *The New Yorker.* He lumped the book into a portmanteau review with Franz Werfel's *Song of Bernadette* ("fascinating") and a book called *A Little Lower Than the Angels* by Virginia Sorenson ("a first novel written with passion and a sense of style"). In contrast, he found Mary McCarthy's first novel to have "the definite attraction of high-grade, backfence gossip." Meg was "characterless, the familiar type that Pearl Harbor has, let us hope, dated completely." And then he delivered the *coup de grace* in a tone of flat, papal infallibility: "Mary McCarthy is no novelist." One of Fadiman's critical tenets, apparently, that if it is possible to recognize a part or a whole of a character the novel is therefore valueless, is echoed by the critic of *The New Republic* at the time, who criticized the book for revealing too much about its author. Her treatment of Jim Barnett, he claimed, was "self-castigatory." She despised the liberal journalist because she knew him too well and his middle-class opinions were essentially her own. Fadiman's further error, confusing the *search* for unity for *lack* of it in her characters, is shared by a number of critics, but he goes on to further confusion by deciding that her talent is wholly lacking in creative force. Her only talent is "for dissecting people and leaving a nasty mess on the table." There *is* a mess left on the psychiatrist's couch, but it is touching, revelatory, open, honest and self-denigratory. It is rather a notable fictional treasure hunt—the search for the self amid all the welter of appearances, pretense, and human contact.

By the time the book was reissued in England in 1957, the *Times Literary Supplement* critic had come around to Mary McCarthy's side. "These six stories are among the most brilliant satiric portraits of modern fiction." Here, almost for the first time in connection with this book, this critic notices her *style,* a notice it became fashionable to take of her subsequent work over and above the subject matter or the ideas. "She writes well *but* . . ." became a favorite critical gambit. The *Times Literary Supplement* says "one admires her wit and her considered, self-conscious yet fluidly elegant style," and then goes on to wonder whether her satire is true, whether satiric exposure of what is should not include an indication of what should be. I will consider the question of the "failure" of satire later; it is enough to say here that *The Company She Keeps* kept company with the best fiction of the early Forties, had no trouble finding friends when it reappeared in the late Fifties, and is still, in the second half of the Sixties, available in paperback, an eminently readable and moving book, beautifully written, and wearing its years surprisingly well.

* * *

There was considerable doubt about whether or not *The Company She Keeps* was a novel. A series of stories held together by a metamorphosing heroine seemed to some critics not to qualify. One called it "thinly disguised autobiography," a good and amusing parallel to the critic who was later to call *Memories of a Catholic Girlhood* thinly disguised fiction. Whether or not the stories added up to a novel, they stood well alone, and in the years between this book and the next, a number of other short stories appeared, among them "The Company Is Not Responsible," in *The New Yorker* in 1944 and "The Unspoiled Reaction" two years later in the *Atlantic Monthly.* These are not especially significant; they might better be described as sketches with a slight core of emotion suggested to the reader but not fully communicated, so removed that the reader has the curious sense that he is being told at second hand about the events. The narrator stands in his way.

"The Company Is Not Responsible" tells of a bus trip the author took from New York to Wellfleet during World War II. After an initial cataloguing of the persons aboard, and a wait until the connecting bus arrives, the bus moves on toward Provincetown. The author listens to the unusual "lark" spirit of the war years, the good-naturedness of the sailor, the girls, Margie and Ann, the Harvard boys, a man named George, the driver called Mac, and the others, but she waits with some dread for the inevitable "detestable person," the "disagreeableness, the bad part" that often breaks out when diverse persons are grouped together and confined.

A near-crisis is reached (although only in the mind of the author) when the Harvard boys begin to sing "Die Lorelei" in German. " 'Will someone object?' I thought; 'is this where the trouble will come?' I held my breath, but no patriot censor intervened." On the contrary, the others join in singing, even the "outsider" author. The boys get off at their stop, bidding everyone good-bye by name, everyone but the author: "I felt a slight stab of envious regret that they did not know my name." Once at home, she begins to disbelieve in the brief experience, until on the return trip she hears George's voice, sees Margie in the crowded bus, and knows her short acquaintanceship with human goodness was not something she "had made up." Slight as the story is, it suggests the changing moods of dread, exultation, distrust, and relief that things are not always as bad as one expects them to be. The form of the sketch is prophetic, a group of persons sequestered for a brief span of time in a limited space, and then observed carefully for their reactions, a form to be used again in *The Oasis, The Groves of Academe, A Charmed Life* and finally in *The Group*. The location of the author is interesting too: the outsider, regretting her stance, feeling disconnected from the group and yet harboring a yearning to be part of it, fearing its potential ugliness yet left with a nostalgia for its unexpected goodness. It is the only example, in Mary McCarthy's work, of a small Eden preserved. Her skepticism was to create a number of other idylls, but "the bad part" always comes upon them.

Another story, "The Unspoiled Reaction," has, oddly enough, been reprinted in a collection called *Masters and Masterpieces of the Short Story*. Whatever the truth of the first part of this title for Mary McCarthy, the second part does not, clearly, apply to this story; it is in no sense a masterpiece. The title refers to what is expected of children at a puppet show, what indeed does occur. The sketch contains the curious, disembodied voice of the narrator, presumably the author who, with her young son, is present at a puppet performance of Little Red Riding Hood in a shabby, near-empty theatre in New York on a rainy Monday morning. The sketch is told, without internal evidence of the presence of the author, and this gives it the same removed feeling I have mentioned, as if emotion were perceived from a great distance. Here primitive fear of a mad, unexplained emotion, suddenly let loose, is felt immediately by both the children, their parents, but only at a distance by the reader. A child in the audience, urged on by his teacher, approaches the puppet and an hysterical human voice, not the falsetto of the puppet, inexplicably frightened by the child's approach, screams out, "You horrible, horrible children," and chases him from the stage. Parents and children are routed from the theatre, the sentence of the outraged teacher ringing in their ears: "That is no way to talk to a *child.*" The story ends with the observation that the sentence is "pronounced by the teacher in a tone of peculiar piety and reverence, her voice genuflecting to it as to the Host."

What happens in "The Unspoiled Reaction" is that an erratic performer whose job is entertaining children as a puppet cracks up in full view of the audience. Her disguised madness breaks forth and shatters the air of childlike trust that had pervaded the theatre. In a way, what happens in this sketch is precisely what does not happen in "The Company Is Not Responsible," where the threat of unpleasantness and evil (in this case nationalism) is contained by the workings of a spirit of goodwill; here, despite the presence of well-meaning parents and "unspoiled" children, evil (madness) breaks through, horrifyingly. "The Unspoiled Reaction" is close in spirit to *The Oasis,* and might almost be said to be a preparatory sketch for it. But the story lacks direction and focus. Its suddenly-revealed moment of emotion is given no explanation, no roots, and few results. It *is*, it threatens the peace of mind of those present, and ultimately the reader's. Nothing more.

Most curious of all is the final sentence I have quoted which seems a simile out of all proportion to the event. The effect of it is that at the very last moment a new note is sounded, a high reverence for the shattered children, and the sudden, new direction of the story stuns the reader. Here, perhaps, its use was incongruous, but this kind of religious imagery crops up often in Mary McCarthy's writing, under all sorts of conditions. In *The Company She Keeps* the safety pin in Meg's underwear seemed to her to be like "a symbol of moral fastidiousness, just as the sores of a mendicant saint can, if thought of in the right way, testify to his moral health." The reliance upon religious imagery, we shall see, becomes even more frequent in the novels to come.

IV *The Facts of Her Fiction*

INTERVIEWER: *Do you object to people playing the* roman à clef *game with your novels?*

MMcC: *I suppose I really ask for it, in a way.*

—*Paris Review,* 1961

IN 1943 and 1944, following the critical approval (and the relatively small sale) that greeted *The Company She Keeps,* the Wilsons spent their winters in New York, their summers in their house in Wellfleet on the Cape. Edmund Wilson had become the full-time, regular book critic for *The New Yorker,* and Reuel was now in kindergarten. In the summer of 1944 there occurred another serious rift in the structure of their marriage, already severely tried by a number of small matters. The story can be found in Mary McCarthy's testimony before the judge hearing her separation petition:

> We had about eighteen people [later she corrected this to "twenty-eight"] at the party. Everybody had gone home and I was washing dishes. I asked him [Wilson] if he would empty the garbage. He said, "Empty it yourself." I started carrying out two large cans of garbage. As I went through the screen door, he made an ironical bow, repeating, "Empty

> it yourself." I slapped him—not terribly hard—went out and emptied the cans, then went upstairs. He called me and I came down. He got up from the sofa and took a terrible swing and hit me in the face and all over. He said: "You think you're unhappy with me. Well, I'll give you something to be unhappy about." I ran out of the house and jumped into my car.

This is, of course, only one side of the testimony, and of interest here only because it appears again, in somewhat different form, in *A Charmed Life,* a novel which was published in 1955, ten years after the marriage was over, but which draws on this marriage for some details:

> Their penultimate quarrel, for example, had exploded in the middle of the night, after a party, when she was carrying two overflowing pails of garbage and he refused, with a sardonic bow, to hold open the screen door for her. There she was, manifestly the injured party, but instead of leaving it at that, and taxing him with it the next day, when he was weakened with a hangover, she immediately distributed the guilt by setting down one pail of garbage and slapping him across his grinning face.

The fact of the matter is that soon after the garbage pail episode Mary McCarthy fled to New York, although *not* in her nightgown as one of the episodes in *A Charmed Life* suggested, and then, like the woman in "The Weeds" (a story in *Cast a Cold Eye*), and perhaps for the same reasons, she came back. In the fall of 1945 the three of them moved back to New York, this time to a house on Henderson Place, and Reuel entered St. Bernard's School. The reunion was only temporary; the winter marked the end of the stormy seven-year marriage. Taking Reuel, she moved to the Stanhope Hotel, making the separation final. Edmund Wilson left for Europe to begin a tour as a correspondent, and separation proceedings were instituted. Later Mary and her son took over her brother Kevin's apartment on East 56th Street, he being in the Army and his wife traveling on tour with a play. Because she has a way of seeing luck or chance as playing a major role in the events of her life, it is notable that on the night she left Edmund Wilson she met for the first time Bowden Broadwater—who was to be her third husband—at a friend's apartment.

That Miles Murphy in *A Charmed Life* is entirely Edmund Wilson is of course clearly untrue; he is less than gossip makes him and more, I suspect, than Mary McCarthy will acknowledge. She says: "Miles is drawn from some Irishman named Miles Something, beginning with an M. The man was someone I'd met very casually but who had red hair. I think I used his physical image . . . I can't think whom he married —someone who used to be my secretary very briefly, I think."

The disclaimer notwithstanding, Miles Murphy continues to remind the reader of Edmund Wilson. Mary McCarthy seems reluctant to write complete fictions or has rarely seemed to conceive of completely imaginary characters. Whether she is conscious of the process or not she shores up her portraits with facts that are indispensable to her *because* they are true. She herself has admitted that even so small a matter as the verisimilitude of names is often a *sine qua non* in her fiction. In an unimportant passage of stray shipboard conversation, in a novel now in progress, she discovered that she had used the names of her two uncles, Frank and Harold. "I *could not* change those names . . . you feel that these names, which have a certain flavor to you, permeate the whole thing like a stain, and maybe this comes through in some mysterious way. Maybe these constellations in real life *do* carry their aura and are transmissible."

This may well explain why, as a novelist, she stays so close to fact, transposing and composing from many real sources but never moving far from what is or was. Miles' and Martha's cross tales about each other, in *A Charmed Life,* his violence toward her, his great, self-involved, self-absorbed intelligence ("Edmund gets the whole household involved in whatever he's doing. He tends to lecture rather than converse, and he'll lecture all through dinner—even all through lunch if he happens to come out for lunch," she once told an interviewer), Miles' inconsistencies of behavior, his enormous erudition and brilliant mind seem to be suggestive of Edmund Wilson.

Later, speaking directly of Edmund Wilson, she summed him up: "He was two people. One is this humanistic Princetonian critic and the other is a sort of minotaur, really, with his terror and pathos." She writes that Martha was terrified of Miles: "Nobody, except Miles, had ever browbeat her successfully" and again, "with Miles she had done steadily what she hated, starting from the moment she married him, violently against her will."

Mary McCarthy says there are no autobiographical elements in *A Charmed Life* except the return of the Sinnotts to New Leeds after Martha's divorce from Miles, and while Miles and his new wife and child are still living there. Note also that, even when she is attempting camouflage, she cannot bring herself to depart very far from originals. The very clear half-step from Wellfleet to New Leeds (the place of *A Charmed Life*) cannot be missed. "What was really autobiographical was this business of coming back in the sense that one had done something wrong that everybody was busy telling you wasn't wrong and you couldn't give a good reason why. . . . But yet I had this sense that it was something I shouldn't have done. . . ."

Both she and Edmund Wilson say they see no resemblance between Miles and Wilson. Edmund Wilson points out that he looks nothing whatever like Miles. Mary McCarthy enumerates a number of differences between the two: Miles has been a boxer, Wilson is utterly unathletic; Miles smokes, Wilson doesn't; Miles has been a philosopher of sorts, Wilson is not interested in philosophy. But the facts of the situation are what have compelled the identification. Mary McCarthy and her third husband *did* return to Wellfleet to live where Mary McCarthy's second husband lived and where she had lived with him, and there are other details, as we have seen, which allow the identification to be made or at least explain why it has been made.

Confronted by the fact that the resemblance was universally noticed ("by people who know nothing about it," she points out), she explains the portrait as a kind of literary legerdemain: "In some sort of joking way, it was as if I were saying to Edmund: 'Look what would happen to you if you were transposed by an evil fairy into this ghastly red-headed, self-analytic, jargon-speaking Irishman. This is what you'd be like. Can you recognize yourself?' Almost a kind of a piece of animism . . . in a sense, the likeness to him would be something only he would recognize."

When the book appeared, and realizing that people were considering it to be a portrait, she wrote to Wilson that she hoped he understood it was *not* intended to be. He wrote back saying that he had not read the book but "I assume it is just another of your malignant, red-haired Irishmen." Wilson was referring to Henry Mulcahy, the monstrous hero of *The Groves of Academe* which had appeared three years before *A Charmed Life*.

In the summer of 1945 Mary McCarthy and Reuel went back to Truro, and Bowden Broadwater visited her there. Apparently, this was an idyllic summer in her personal life and a crucial one in her political thinking. More and more she and her friends were concerned about the war and its consequences for European intellectuals. On the sands of Truro her friendship with Nicola Chiaromonte began, there she, Dwight Macdonald, the novelist Niccolò Tucci, Lionel Abel, and others formed a kind of informal literary group, reading Shakespeare aloud, the kind of thing Mary McCarthy liked to do from earlier days. (Another reading group of this sort had James Farrell in it.) A fictional appearance of this fondness of hers for being part of an active, literary community is the reading group in *A Charmed Life* that gets together to "do" *Bérénice,* purely imaginary in the novel but true to her own life. That summer, sand seeping into her typewriter, she worked on a translation of the French philosopher Simone Weil's *Iliad, or, The Poem of Force,* which appeared as *politics* Pamphlet No. 1 in April 1947, after appearing earlier in the magazine itself.

Faced with the prospect of a single life again, she decided to try her hand at teaching. In the fall she went to Bard College at Annandale-on-Hudson on the recommendation of F. W. Dupee, a friend who was teaching there at the time, putting Reuel into Upper Red Hook School, a public school close by. Her only other teaching experience, aside from this year at Bard, was to be at Sarah Lawrence College in 1948 for a single semester.

Of her brief experiences in teaching Mary McCarthy has said that she "adored" teaching at Bard . . ." but the students were so poor at Sarah Lawrence that I did not enjoy it there. . . . But at Bard it was very exciting. . . . I had never taught before, and I was staying up till two in the morning every night trying to keep a little bit ahead of my class." She remembers, however, being greatly frightened of the whole unaccustomed ordeal of teaching. "My first day, I learned later, my students thought I might faint and that they'd have to carry me out. I was so scared. It didn't occur to *me* that I might faint but I must have turned very white." Bard's experimental system bothered her. The instructor was often somewhat "behind" a student tutee who was working in a field the instructor did not know much about. This system produced either total exhaustion for the teacher at the end of the year, or a real impetus toward intensive study ("I liked teaching because I loved this business of studying") or, in Mary McCarthy's case, both. The enduring results of these short excursions into academia were *The Groves of Academe,* a number of critical essays on literature, which we may assume grew out of, or at least began with, the close, wide reading of those years, and two scholarly books of art history and criticism which testify to a genuine and continuing taste for scholarship.

The world at large knows what Mary McCarthy thought of Vassar, of Bard and, most explicitly, is aware of her lack of respect for the students, faculty, curriculum and general climate of Sarah Lawrence. What she was like on the campus of Sarah Lawrence, what her colleagues thought of her, can only be surmised from the one piece of possible evidence, this a novel by the late Randall Jarrell published in 1960 and called *Pictures from an Institution.* Jarrell—poet, critic, and novelist—taught at Sarah Lawrence, Mary McCarthy knew him, although he was not at Sarah Lawrence at the same time she was. Yet her detractors are united in their view that Gertrude in that novel is the spit and image of Mary McCarthy.

On the surface, as the subject herself is quick to point out, the resemblances are not striking. Gertrude Johnson is homely, addicted to eating sweets, satirical, a woman of atrocious taste in homemaking and dressing, a terrible housekeeper who "had taught writing once at an old-fashioned high schoolish college in Missouri." She is Southern, a novelist "between novels," and a notably poor cook; the meal she serves to the President and a few faculty members is a masterpiece of inedibility. Mary McCarthy says of the fictional portrait:

> It didn't resemble me in any way that counted. . . . If I had seen some of my characteristics, I think if he had written something that involved my appearance in a way that was unpleasant for me to see, my *real* appearance, not that I was short, fat, bad-skinned etc., which I knew I wasn't, if he'd involved my character that I recognized, then perhaps I would have suffered. . . .

She adds that when the book appeared she wrote to Jarrell concerning another matter, the anti-Joseph McCarthy magazine she wanted to start, and said she had heard "that Gertrude was supposed to be me, and that I didn't think so. He wrote back and said, 'No, it's me,—you know, like Flaubert." Anthony West, reviewing the book in *The New Yorker,* was of the same mind. He wrote that the book "arouses in this reader . . . the sort of dismay aroused by those oils in which the artist is discovered solemnly painting himself."

That this was a literary jest Jarrell was making to Mary McCarthy seems obvious. Gertrude was the *object* of Jarrell's scorn, his most acid attack and, like Henry Mulcahy in *The Groves of Academe,* becomes under his pen a monster in the feminine gender. Gertrude does seem to gather together under one skin many views of Mary McCarthy that have been expressed by "enemies" (a word she herself uses often for them):

> She wore her hair more or less as our mothers wore it; her features . . . were undistinguished. Then one noticed that she had an obstinate Irish . . . upper lip.

[On seeing the President of Benton College] She realized she was no longer between novels. She looked at the President as a weary, wayworn diamond prospector looks at a vein of blue, volcanic clay.

The Robbins and the Whitakers were there [at Gertrude's] because they were going to be in Gertrude's book about Benton. Gertrude was never polite to anything but material; when she patted someone on the head, you could be sure that the head was about to appear, smoked, in her next novel.

What a memory Gertrude had! . . And how tone deaf! She had never heard a tune.

[Her home is Bleecker Street in Greenwich Village. She listens As A Novelist, she lives with her third husband, Sidney, who exists to serve her alone, and who had] "married her for her books," [and to whom she murmurs after every party,] "Aren't they *dull,* Sidney?"

[She is a] thorough Freudian . . . a continually witty and occasionally humorous woman. She loved to make people laugh, just as she loved to shock them.

[And her smile, occasion for a long paragraph] She was a mousy woman till she smiled: her teeth bared themselves, counted, their lips went over them. Her smile was all that people have called it: it was like a skull, like a stone-marten scarf, like catatonia . . . And yet it was only a nervous grimace. . . .

She did not tell people at Benton she was writing a book about them: it would make them nervous if they knew. [Her passion is for *facts.* He has her say]: Tell me some Facts. Some facts about —— [And having heard them from the poet she talks about the college in wit-laden, McCarthy-like sentences] Americans are so conformist that even their dissident groups exhibit the most abject conformity. [And she goes on, with what seems now almost like a remarkable

> piece of foresight] A Group for Everyone and Everyone in His Group is the slogan of their sampler.
>
> Benton College is a surprisingly contented place . . . Gertrude could see all this about Benton, but she was unwilling to believe it, and she had a theoretical manipulative skill by which she could explain it or anything else away . . . [Her books were] crushed down into method: as I read I was so conscious of what was being done that I scarcely noticed or cared what it was being done to. . . .
>
> Gertrude had labored carefully to mock, lament, and execrate—to condemn utterly, and to do so it had also been necessary for her to understand, for her to have at the tips of her fingernails the Facts. [And later, on the subject of her style: claiming that memory is the Mother of the Muses,] Gertrude was as knowing as *Time*. All clichés, slogans, fashions, turns of speech, details of dress, disguises of affection, tunnels or by-passes of ideology, gravestones of rationalization and cant lived in Gertrude as though in a nutrient broth . . . If one of Gertrude's heroines, running to snatch from the lips of her little daughter a half-emptied bottle of furniture polish, fell and tore her skirt, Gertrude knew the name of the dressmaker who had made the skirt—and it was the right name for a woman of that class, at that date; she knew the brand of the furniture polish. . . .

If Mary McCarthy could not recognize the portrait (she says that she never looks for material, admits she is tone-deaf—as are many other writers—and points out that she is anti-Freudian) and Randall Jarrell disclaimed it, the reader detects some satiric assaults upon and distortions of her characteristics as a novelist. Her propensity for the fact in fiction, her affection for catalogues, her wit and sharpness of attack when she feels the need to attack, her customary resort to the people she knows well for her characters: all these ring true. The brief semester at Sarah Lawrence served Randall

Jarrell well, it would seem; it and the year at Bard served *her* equally well in *The Groves of Academe.*

At the end of the Bard year, and suffering from an assortment of illnesses brought on by the killing pace of academic life in an experimental college, she spent the summer in Europe where, this time by design, she met Bowden Broadwater in Paris. (Reuel was spending the summer with his father at the Cape.) This was the first summer after the end of the War and, needing a journalist's card to travel in Europe, she got one from *Town and Country,* for whom she wrote a travel piece. Mary McCarthy and Bowden Broadwater traveled together to Italy; an account of this trip is in the story, "The Cicerone," which *Partisan Review* published. In the fall she returned to New York, Reuel came back to her and returned to St. Bernard's School.

Their problem now was housing. After staying briefly at a poor hotel, and unable to find an apartment, they moved in with Broadwater and his sister. "Perhaps I didn't look as hard as I should have . . it's amazing how one didn't think about conventions very much at that age."

Broadwater was thin, eccentric, and boyish. He had had an excellent education at the best schools and was, at that time, unemployed. "There was something physically attractive about him, certainly, very pretty skin and gold hair but very, very nearsighted with very large spectacles that gave him a strange, tense look," she says. The portrait of her Young Man traveling companion in "The Cicerone" and the resemblance to Bowden Broadwater of John Sinnott of *A Charmed Life* reiterate her view that he was something of a snob. He really was, she says, "intensely snobbish." He was as well a somewhat talented if blocked writer who had written and published a few stories but found writing so agonizing an experience that he was able to produce very little. "But he was tremendously talented, much more talented than I."

One story he did write, in 1948, and which was later published in the *Paris Review,* concerned their first ménage together on East 57th Street. No elegant abode, as the address might suggest, it was a small place, heated by self-lit gas radiators, with a bathtub in the kitchen. The tiny space inhabited by four persons made Reuel nickname the apartment "the Anthill," but Mary McCarthy remembers it as "a great deal of fun."

Finally, in December, they were married. The legal separation from Wilson had by now become a divorce, but marriage to Broadwater did not seem a pressing affair until a visiting friend questioned the propriety of the household, especially from Reuel's point of view. At that point, she and Broadwater married. The following summer the two of them were in Vermont at a borrowed house in Pawlet, and Reuel visited them there, the main part of the summer being again spent with Edmund Wilson. This summer place is the geographic setting of her second novel, *The Oasis;* the events that suggested the theme of that book were occurring at about the same time.

In New York in the fall of 1947, Broadwater found a job, almost a hack job, working for a medical digest, a job for which he was unsuited and which did not last long. He then went to work for *Partisan Review,* for which his wife was still writing her "Theatre Chronicle." On the side they both became involved with other New York intellectuals, Philip Rahv among them, in a deep concern for the shape of the postwar world. Much talk, with reference to Arthur Koestler's theory of "oases" and a sense of obligation to the non-Communist left-wing intellectuals in Europe, led them to form an organization they called Europe-America Groups. Their idea was to raise money to send abroad to these persons who were isolated between the Communists, on the one hand, and the American-supported power structure, on the other. It was, remembers Mary McCarthy, "a completely harmless" organization, but bitter factionalism developed within it, to a point where one group, it was rumored, was trying to make off with the organization's treasury.

This experience, or disillusion, is the basis for *The Oasis.* In the spring of 1948, now teaching at Sarah Lawrence and commuting from New York to Bronxville, she began to write the book. She continued working on it that summer after Sarah Lawrence while she and her husband were staying in Cornwall, Connecticut. Published first in *Horizon,* under the title *A Source of Embarrassment,* it won the *Horizon* prize and appeared as the complete issue of that magazine in February 1949. Cyril Connolly said of it in his introduction that it was the kind of book "which *Horizon* exists to further . . . We are back in our own difficult, restricted, avant-garde mental climate."

The Oasis is another group study or what might be called a community novel, a favorite form for Mary McCarthy. This may be because she found it convenient to "study" characters so grouped together. Time, as in the chronicle novel for example, is not the catalyst; instead characters confined in a geographical area act and react upon each other. Also, the group novel allows us to watch a number of diverse persons on stage at once, and their special characteristics make a complex and fascinating tapestry. We have a chance to stare a long time, and nothing changes much before our eyes. It is almost plotless, and in its static form and in the strongly allegorical nature of its characters, it is indeed what its author said it was to the editor of *Horizon,* "a landscape with figures, the figures being treated realistically, in a sort of Piero della Francesca manner, and the landscape being, on the one hand, an idyllic Nature, and on the other, a strange political climate of the real which they fantastically inhabit." We are able to watch, as well, a genuine intelligence deal with intellectuals, with all the force of what John Chamberlain has called her "disenchanted common sense."

If there was doubt that *The Company She Keeps* was a "true" novel, there was even more about *The Oasis.* Cyril Connolly acknowledged that "perhaps she lacked narrative power"; and to the *Paris Review* interviewer she later said bluntly: "*The Oasis* is not a novel . . . I never meant it to be. It's a *conte, a conte philosophique.*" Even *conte* seems somewhat exaggerated. It is more accurate to describe it by using her earlier image, a still life or tableau, or even a charade, a philosophical landscape of fantastical quality inhabited by allegorical figures. The title, she has said, comes from Arthur Koestler, who suggested the possibilities of establishing oases—small libertarian groups that would try "to change the world on a small scale."

The events of the book are these: a group of American intellectuals (all, that is, except the businessman Joe Lockman and his sybaritic wife, Eva) buy an abandoned summer hotel on a mountaintop in New England. Their aim is to retreat from atomic warfare (the time is the future but close enough to the present to be recognizable), to accomplish a "secession from society" into a Utopia composed of civilized, educated persons. The Utopians are divided into two diverse ways of thought. The purists are led by Macdougal Macdermott, the editor of a libertarian magazine, "ordinarily a serious-minded man, ready to oppose sectarianism whenever he observed it in others . . puritanical, disputatious, hard-working, monogamous, a good father and a good friend." Will Taub, who is Jewish and sensitive about it, leads the other faction, the realists, who "had accepted as their historic mission the awakening of the left to the dangers of Red totalitarianism." There are others, notably Susan Hapgood, "a young novelist . . . loving only books and conversation." She is possessed of a "plain, small-town voice . . . an inordinate curiosity" and "small-town courtesy." Taub's Gentile wife, Cynthia, "a reserved girl who designed clothes" and "spoke very little at parties"; Katy Norell, a charming, sensitive and vulnerable young woman, and her husband, Preston ("He thought of Utopia simply as a place in which it would be impossible ever to escape from her, a multiplication of marriage or its projection into eternity"). There is Eleanor Macdermott, who "had been born into New York society, and though a gentle disposition and an identification with the unfortunate had given her pretty, slight form and fragile pastel features that downtrodden and even necessitous appearance so common among charitable women, she still expressed herself in the secure manner of one who enjoyed advantages." And there are others, of both parties, who appear on occasion: a Catholic "Latinist teacher of boys, a Protestant clergyman, a trade union publicist, several high-school teachers, an alcoholic woman illustrator," among others.

Three crises of rising intensity strike the Utopians. The first two are brought about by the "simple-souled, commonsensical" Joe Lockman, the leather-goods entrepreneur whose election to Utopia is hotly debated among the prospective colonists until the two factions are shamed into accepting him by a blunt question from Eleanor Macdermott: "What is Utopia but the right to an human existence?" Joe, the well-meaning, unthinking, diabetic bourgeois, shakes the colony again early in its establishment by putting an ancient stove out of commission and later frightening Taub with an unexpected prod of his shotgun. ("Practical jokes were anathema to him [Taub]; they belonged to an order of things which defied his powers of anticipation, like children, birds, cows, water, snakes, lightning, Gentiles, and automobiles.") Only the humor of the situation and the ridiculousness of the protestants break up the meeting to oust him. But the major, final crisis is not his doing. It comes from outside the group. Established, prosperous and economically secure, the community plans a strawberry picnic only to find that some interlopers, a woman, child and man speaking "in a gruff accent they did not recognize" have driven into the patch and are picking their berries. When Cynthia and Will approach tentatively, politely, they neither look up nor reply. "The pickers appeared to be of the very poorest farmer class." Katy tries speaking reasonably to them. "The man muttered something, and they all stopped picking for a moment, with surly but tentative expressions as though waiting." Politely Cynthia inquires: " 'Won't you leave some for us, please?' . . . At this the man snorted, emboldened, it seemed, by her nervousness, and raised his hand abruptly in a rude and half-menacing gesture." She walks away, hearing "the woman's shrill voice behind her shouting obscene imprecations." Preston and "the young divine" in the colony take Joe's shotgun and frighten the "brutal people" off.

This minuscule "threat" spells the end of the colony. "Ultimately Utopia would fail; that was to be expected. But it might survive for many months or for years, if the production of a commodity more tangible than morality could be undertaken. Morality did not keep well. . . ."

The book has two noticeable strengths: its style and its "ideas." It is studded with the right words, witty phrases, epithets and sentences that can be called "fine." Even her dependent clauses are barbed: "With that instinctive tactlessness so common among educated people," is a fair example. Her sentences tend to rise up and strike: "The ease with which his arguments were prevailing awoke him to question their validity." Occasionally, however, her unerring taste and accuracy fails as is inevitable with any writer who aims so many arrows at such diverse targets. Susan, walking with Taub and spying upon the colonists' belongings as they unpack, sees him looking at a girl's long legs. She "watched them move bulgingly down the tract of his appreciation, like a snake's dinner, to join the Jacksons' English bicycles and the breasts of the minister's wife." Even when it becomes clear that the referent for "them" is the girl's legs, the image seems tasteless and unpalatable. Or again: "Henry, a tall, thin, young man with an ovoid head who resembled a nail file" strains one's ability to form a useful image. Sometimes, moreover, the images are physically painful: "and his heart, as he smoked, grew large with a pure and personal regret," a sentence which might have been acceptable without "as he smoked." There is an occasional overuse of heavy, Latinized words: "a sense of restored continuity soothed his locative anxiety" is a good case in point. These minor complaints accompany one's discomfort with her rather oppressive use of foreign words and phrases (*faute de mieux, lèse majesté, élan, amour-propre, force majeure, malentendu, enceinte,* etc.). This usage customarily marks an impatience with the resources of one's own language, the symptom, often, of youthful style. One feels the presence of a young writer seeking rather disparately for exact, suitable approaches to her meaning.

It is easy to be picayune about a writer's style, to point out the constant elements in it which tend to irritate the reader, and the weaknesses which ring in the ear. I find it far harder to indicate the very real strengths of Mary McCarthy's style. Her undergraduate writing indicates that at the outset she wrote with a strong inclination toward classical prose style. Even this early her sentences are balanced and precise. They tend to be epigrammatic and then to culminate in what might be called a periodic paragraph, the sentences increasing in strength until the last forceful phrase. As the style matured it never changed too much from this basic pattern. The sentences became longer, but still held together by antithesis, by balance, by a careful, structural sense. Her diction leans heavily on latinate and romance words; she has a dislike of slang and never uses it unless it serves (as it does in *The Group*) a narrative purpose. Her writing is rarely ornamental, never poetic; it is notable that she never "paints a landscape" or even is aware, seemingly, of the world of nature in which human beings exist. This contributes to the "allegorical" tone of her fiction. Her prose, deceptively dry at times, then judiciously (and often surprisingly) punctuated with a witty sentence, alternately abstract (in the classical manner) and then graphically concrete, is coherent, consciously structured to give her ideas and observations the greatest force. She is fond of the unsupportable generalization ("Like all European women, she. . . . ") if it serves her satiric purpose, even fonder of the supportable, accurate detail.

If her paragraphs are periodic in form, the rhythm rising toward the final period, so too are her chapters. Often she will bring a whole book to a climax in the last paragraph, whipping it all to a fine, final classical fury with a Latin quotation, or she will close by bringing up the big guns of a final paradox (as in *The Groves of Academe* and *A Charmed Life*), aware, in the twist of a sentence, of the irony of human existence and the vagaries of human thought.

As for its ideas, *The Oasis* might be described as a declaration of lack of faith, a set of articles of disbelief. If Mary McCarthy had once put her trust in the Left, in radical parties of that persuasion, she here seems to separate herself from that trust; if belief in a unified and dogmatic system of thought had ever held her she here publicly abandons it; and if she ever thought that the American liberal was closer to an effective morality than the American reactionary or moderate she here throws doubts upon *that* assumption. Her own liberal stance does not save her from a profound distrust of liberals and intellectuals: "They were grateful to Eleanor Macdermott for saving them from an act of ostracism which would indeed have been an ugly beginning for a community devoted to brotherhood." And then: "All had counted on the virtues of others to rescue them from themselves." She reflects her distrust of the colonists' motives, their force, their ability to make effective decisions, their honesty. When they do act the result is usually self-destructive or harmful to those they profess to love: "No murderers or thieves applied [for admission to Utopia], only ordinary people of ordinary B plus morality, people whose crimes that is, had been confined to an intimate circle, and who had never injured anybody but a close friend, a relation, a wife, a husband, themselves."

There is no fury, no passionate resentment born of disappointment in Mary McCarthy's attitude towards her characters in Utopia, although she says the book grew out of her fury at her experience with Europe-America Groups. She regards them coolly, with detachment, and her ear for their tonal vacillations, their distress with themselves, their self-justifying inner dishonesty is unerring. If her memory, as some critics have insisted, has served her too well (indicating the very real resemblance of Will Taub to Philip Rahv and

Macdougal Macdermott to Dwight Macdonald) it may also be that these "facts" of character are part of the strength of the book. She herself does not hesitate to say that "they were all, more or less, straight portraits, not even composites." Particularly angry critics, like Margaret Marshall, her former collaborator on *The Nation,* pinned their criticisms on these identifications, as if being able to "spot" the originals of a literary character automatically made the fictional portraits valueless. Mary McCarthy's portraits, said Miss Marshall, are clever and malicious, she "has no qualms about using her best friends and closest associates as material for her fiction," and the result is that *The Oasis* "is not serious . . . either as a work of art or as the satiric comment it purports to be on our contemporary intellectual and political life." Donald Barr in *The Times* said that readers outside "her inner circle" would "get little from *The Oasis* except a vague sense of defamatory brilliance and a few fine scenes." Gorham Munson put the same point more gently by saying that she was "too close to her material, too much identified with it herself." Few of these critics have cared to say what the effect of the book might possibly be upon the outsider or to hazard a guess as to what it may be upon a generation for whom knowledge of the "originals" is completely lost. Are they likely, not knowing who Taub and Macdermott and the others are supposed to be, to feel excluded from the book? Is the force of the satire really affected or diminished by this knowledge or the lack of it? I doubt it. Certainly her literary acquaintance with liberalism must of necessity stem from her knowledge of liberals. And though later she will reiterate her belief in "a kind of libertarian socialism, a decentralized socialism," she had long ago lost her faith in the kind of persons that might have been expected to accomplish these ends or would at least have professed a strong interest in their achievement.

Mary McCarthy knew these people well; on one level, indeed, it *is* a *roman à clef,* but it goes further. The book is a series of flashes of instant recognition into their motives, their vacillations, their character. Just as there is no plot, no important events that proceed one from another, so there is no development of character or even any real change in the characters. They are satiric portraits, brilliantly placed like precious stones into a setting. Their failures, or what might be termed their sins, are intellectual, their virtues are the negative ones, their attractions for the reader are their patent weaknesses. Our attitude becomes the author's as, in an unusual abdication of her own faith in liberalism, we react with her. We feel skepticism, some amusement, slight dismay, and acute embarrassment, all cerebral reactions to what is, after all, a book of ideas. We suspend ourselves and our private views of the liberal, intellectual person long enough to accept hers, like the congregation of a popular minister who willingly follow his political, economic and aesthetic views because they are so completely "with" him on theological matters. In the case of *The Oasis,* one of these newly accepted attitudes is the author's developing attitude toward men, sex and love. In *The Company She Keeps* we saw her begin to put down her amusement at sex, the Fall become a pratfall, the sense of the ridiculous that finally overcomes Meg's horror the morning after in Mr. Breen's compartment. Although sex as such plays no part in what happens in *The Oasis,* and there are no seductions and no one "takes" anyone even once, there are hints that Mary McCarthy still has found no reason to take sex or marriage seriously. Eva Lockman, watching her aging husband become excited at a suggestion made at a community meeting, says to the minister's wife: "He'll pay for it tonight." She refers to "a digestive disturbance, the result of too much excitement," and the author goes on to suggest: "There was an appropriateness, seized though not fully analyzed by Eva, in the fact that Joe's body, which he refused to coddle, should prove her ally, and her allusions to its behavior suggested a wealth of knowledge more intimate and exclusive than love." A little further on, Leo, one of the book's more likable intellectuals, cataloguing for Joe the impossible, impractical suggestions in history, says: "Sex surely must have been the first. What a ludicrous action if looked at from a rational standpoint."

If sex continues to have the shape of the ludicrous, an entertainment that more closely resembles vaudeville (with its pratfalls) than romance or drama, marriage is seen to be a trap or a war that serves at every turn to remind its principals of their embattled, ensnared state. Preston Norell reacts to the episode of the flooded stove, in which his wife had an innocent part: "This [thinking of Katy and his mother] produced in him the disagreeable sensation of having been born married... a nomadic and restless temperament, he had felt a deep-going antipathy to Utopia and the suggestions of finality it conveyed." Katy thinks of their relationship in terms of battle: "The armies of love rushed after him, to surrender and bring him back captive. To surrender and treat afterwards was Katy's habitual strategy in love," and of marriage as a private battlefield: "That the privacy to make a scene was something she would miss in Utopia was a contingency she had never anticipated... she felt deprived of a basic right... He [Preston] felt protected by the others... and a cruel streak in his character was rejoiced by this turning of the tables... little had she thought, when urging on him the manifold blessings of Utopia, that *this* would prove to be the chief."

Mary McCarthy's role as "ironical word-lover" (this is Cyril Connolly's phrase) is apparent in these few sentences. She is equally divided, it would seem, between the stylist she is and the "wrecker," the deflater of thought in fictional form. So tough-minded and distrustful is she of the ideas she allows to roam free through this book that one begins to doubt that this is a novel at all. It is, rather, a display case for the death of certain illusions, among them that liberalism in political theory or action is more reliable than any other philosophy, or that liberals because of their men-of-good-will phrases and high-sounding, resounding talk, are nobler than other men. Joe Lockman comes out of this book rather well, almost the way Mr. Breen did out of "The Man in the Brooks Brothers Shirt." Both are blunt, direct, unpretentious, unintellectual, and likable in contrast to the slippery, pretentious, weak and foolish intellectuals; Meg as antagonist to Breen fits this description of the intellectuals at many points. In this Utopia it is discovered that "a man can live without self-respect, but a group shatters, dispersed by the ugliness it sees reflected in itself." The virtues that survive this pitiless discovery are sparse, individual, and occasional: honesty with one's self, a thin sprinkling of ineffectual yet well-meaning human kindness, a kind of surface *politesse,* and an appetite for the good "not of this world, and not to be satisfied by actions which would forever cheat its insistencies."

The image-lover that Mary McCarthy is here chooses her similes from an already recognized source, her childhood religious training. At least ten times in the short space of less than two hundred pages her references are strongly religious and liturgical. Taub feels a *Te Deum* swelling in his heart, the shadow of the vanished theoretical founder of the community falls on the hillside "comparable to the shadow of Calvary upon the militant Church," and Katy poses as a Pietà. There are many more. The Catholic girlhood may not have sustained her spiritually, but it served her literary needs exceedingly well.

The lover of paradox in her is never stronger than here in this essentially ironic set of circumstances. She writes: "America Last, an anti-war organization so reactionary that it had not yet been certified as disloyal" (a prophetic irony as it turned out), and "pacificism had not yet been made a crime, providing that the pacifist was above the age to bear arms or suffered some physical disability." The larger irony is, of course, the defeat of a group of intellectuals, not by the brutish, almost animal-like intruders, but by the invocation in themselves, at the smallest threat to their property and their appetites, of the most primitive emotions. The beast within takes over at the suggestion of the beast from without, and idealism is dealt a blow.

And while we are at it, it is well to notice the resemblance of the instruments that bring self-knowledge in *The Oasis* to those in two later stories, "The Appalachian Revolution" (1954) and "The Hounds of Summer" (1963). Both stories contain a threat to an idyllic state. In the first a lake, belonging by rights of usage to the "old" summer people, is invaded by "foreign intruders," later revealed to the inhabitants as "psychiatrists" who arrive in "big black cars." One of them is distingushed by a "mop of gray hair," and they all speak in "authoritative foreign" voices; their wives are "mountains of white flesh and bulging veins spilling out of tight new bathing suits, one lavender, one black." All of them "speak loudly, in heavily stressed voices."

In "The Hounds of Summer" the unspoiled nature of a little fishing village in Italy, inhabited in the summer by a congenial group of allies including some Jews, is threatened by the arrival of Germans, "fat, middle-aged blond strangers . . . extremely ugly [who] brought food with them, and ate lunch at midday, scattering grape skins and peach pits and salami rind and crusts of bread on the marble and throwing empty Chinotto bottles into the sea." They speak in "raucous authoritarian voices," they are "old enough to have been in the S.S." Their presence in the village, at the favorite swimming place, throws a pall upon the whole vacation. The place is "spoiled," and there is the feeling that the "old people" will not return to meet the intruders another year.

The Germans and the psychiatrists (who might well be German too although we are not told) are related in kind to the muttering peasants in *The Oasis.* They are all tools or agents of self-knowledge; the "good," sensitive intellectuals are made to realize that their own reactions are horrifying, far worse than the behavior of the brutes, whose characteristics, like the coarse, brutal Nazi in Meg's dream in "Ghostly Father, I Confess," represent a threat to the weakened intellectual only because they throw the intellectual back upon himself and make him aware of his own failures. They are the catalysts of the modern intellectuals' dilemma, hastening his vision of himself and ultimately, therefore, his defeat. If the brutes seem, upon repetition, to be rather simplified figures for fiction, it may be because it is often not fiction that Mary McCarthy is writing but rather an allegorical essay, and the invaders are symbols, not characters. In conversation Mary McCarthy has said that *The Oasis,* "The Hounds of Summer," and "The Appalachian Revolution" are her favorites among her work. This is added evidence that her tendency in fiction is the essayist's, closer to the dealer in ideas, and her affection is for her work that resembles this genre. It testifies as well to her fondness for the idea of "community," the warm in-ness of it, the Group whose exclusiveness is endangered by encroachment. The groups she herself has been part of are intellectually highly selective and close, and *The Oasis* and the stories that follow its pattern suggest some of her doubts about the permanence of these groups, whether threatened from within (as by the realists in *The Oasis*) or from without. This affection for the fictional form of the "community" novel is to influence future work, notably *The Group*.

Some rather acrid controversy revolves around whether or not *The Oasis* is satire. There is no more agreement about this than there is about what satire is. In fact, those who carp at the idea of Mary McCarthy as satirist are capable of holding entirely divergent views as to what it is she fails to be, what requirements she fails to satisfy. As Alvin Kernan has pointed out, satire in our time has an unsavory reputation; even if it is admired it is at the same time resented: "Readers find it embarrassingly ungenerous in its depiction of man, particularly when its harshness is contrasted with the kindly tolerance of comedy or the profound sympathy of tragedy for the failings of human nature." To most contemporaries, the satirist is the least popular of writers because his target is human pretensions, and we hate to watch these being exposed, we flinch from the sight. He is himself most disliked, it has been said, and then attacked, in periods when there is greatest agreement among his readers about the standards they themselves accept. United in their vision of themselves and their standards, they will brook no criticism of these matters, especially when it is tinged with humor. Among a few satirists there is a dual conviction that things were better in the past or that they might possibly improve in some distant future: only the present is terrible. There are, in addition, satirists who project their work into the future to show that, rosy as it is generally thought to be, in itself it promises no improvement whatever; in *no* direction, to them, is there much hope, and they are fond of attacking the idea that we are improving, that society is progressing, that education, culture, civilization have changed man for the better. It is most unpopular to do this. Man lives on illusions about himself, his hopes, his dreams, his resolutions. The satirist who is concerned to destroy these illusions is in trouble with his own time.

Juvenal's famous claim that satire has an interest in anything men do is adequate to define its subject matter, but it leaves the question of attitude or tone undetermined. Northrop Frye thinks wit or humor is essential; attack without humor, or pure denunciation, is quickly dated, he says. "Attack in literature never can be a pure expression of merely personal or even social hatred. . . ." The tone of satire is perhaps skepticism, almost cynicism. Further, the temper of high satire may often bring the satirist close to obscenity. There is also in Frye's view "moral reference" in all great satire. As he says in his essay on satire: "In the long run, the tone of antagonism or attack in satire must imply an assertion and a defense of a moral principle."

Other criteria are suggested by other critics. "There is always at least a suggestion of some kind of humane ideal in satire," says one; another that "the satirist always portrays the grotesque and distorted and concentrates [as Frye has pointed out] to an obsessive degree upon the flesh." Kernan says "we seem in satire always to be at the extreme," which leads, one would suspect, to characters that are flat, all or nothing, one thing and not another. People in satire are not developed in the way that they are in the social or psychological novel, but are extremes, grotesques, forever the same and in this sense, symbolic.

Satire is customarily pessimistic, the pain the satirist feels at what he sees is the *tone*. The method of relieving the pain is mockery. By his tone and his choice of objects for his satire the satirist passes moral judgment on his fellowmen and their behavior. Thus he tends himself to become proud. This "weak" spot in the satirist's private personality is often the point of attack for his critics. His indignation, his dedication to truth, and his pessimism become themselves targets for his incensed readers or his critics. In the attack they launch upon *him,* he is often shown to be less than worthy himself and so open to any attack.

Turning back to Mary McCarthy we see the attacks upon her satire as the result of diverse definitions of satire. The late Joseph Henry Jackson has reproached her with touching "only the reader's mind . . . whereas the genuinely first-rate satiric novel must also touch the reader's emotions." This comment ignores the number of ways in which satire may "touch" the reader, and it interprets it only as "moving" the reader, ignoring the possibility of inaugurating in him a kind of shock of recognition which moves him out of complacency, an epiphany that he may experience at the sight of reality laid bare. Gorham Munson in *The Saturday Review* said that it was the question of distance that disqualified her: she was too much identified with her material herself. Satire is critical, he goes on; Mary McCarthy is more amused than critical, and she takes "a self-sufficient delight in her characters and their dilemmas." Henry Rago felt that her characters were so flat that they "were limited to the kind of caricature you find in the broadest and least subtle forms of satire." And Donald Barr attacks on two fronts:

> There are two types of satire, two ways of developing such an idea as this. One assails our common conceit and folly, analyzing the general nature of man and his institutions. The

> other assails particular figures, relying on the reader's having or wanting the key to "the originals." Great satire is the first.

This division relegates *The Oasis* to a lesser level without any evidence but that favorite device of the daily journalist, a self-made definition under which the work being discussed does not do well at all. Margaret Marshall used the same self-conceived definition approach: "Satire, good satire, breathes hatred of evil and stupidity—but its mainspring is love of the good and the intelligent. It always subsumes a passionate belief in moral values and is therefore affirmation." *The Oasis* fails on all these counts because it "expresses no emotion stronger than condescension or scorn." Louise Bogan is even harsher, demanding "that part of the maturing equipment of the satirist should be warmth," although, after Juvenal and Swift, this seems a curiously limiting requirement. In reviewing a later book of Mary McCarthy's, the same critic says that her satire is never "quite relentless or thorough enough," without pausing to define the limits of satire she has presumably failed to reach.

If these reviewers set up private definitions, like private examinations, and then fail the writer on these grounds, others, like Denham Sutcliffe, flunk her for being *too close* to the classic definition. Quoting Lady Mary Wortley Montague's famous couplet, "Satire should, like a polished razor keen/ Wound with a touch that's scarcely felt or seen," he concludes that in *The Oasis* the touch is not that deft but the razor is too keen, "so keen that it's hard to know what she is satirizing."

If quotation alone would solve the problem, Mary McCarthy might well resort to an old sixteenth-century couplet: "He who satire loves to sing/ On himself will satire bring." Her satire in *The Oasis* is classic, her ideal is human society based upon reason, intelligence and selflessness, her oasis is a fantasy, and her object of attack the pretentiousness and dishonesty (even to themselves and usually to others) of the most intellectual, the selfishness of the most endowed with worldy goods. That she offers little hope for her ideal is in the accepted tradition of the form. It is critically irrelevant to dismiss this classic stance by launching personal attacks upon her use of known persons as models for characters or to accuse her of failing to be "affirmative" or lacking "passionate moral belief." These may indeed be true of her (although to me it is fairly apparent that her destruction of tissues of pretension is fired by fury at moral failures) but in any sense they are no real detriment to successful satire. Her posture in this book is pessimistic, critical and mocking. And so passionately does she advance this position that she might be echoing Juvenal: *"Difficile est saturam non scribere* [It is difficult *not* to write satire]."

Questioned recently on the subject of her use of satire, Mary McCarthy spoke in this way:

> QUERY: Have you considered a definition?
>
> MMcC: Yes, one's forced into it. Perhaps to the classical definition: the distorting mirror held up to society. With the object of amendment of manners and morals? No I think not. This is a gloss, a virtuous gloss.
>
> QUERY: And the tone?
>
> MMcC: Satire invites exaggeration. You can't have it without some sort of distortion. The best satire seems to spring from hatred and repugnance: Swift, Juvenal, Martial, Pope. I resist the notion that there can be such a thing as "gentle satire"—Addison and Steele, Horace. Despite Molière, I keep coming back to satire as a cruel mirror, distorting; it is not a true, gay vision. It *pretends* to be, as though someone slyly pushed you before a trick looking-glass, someone who hated you. Real satire—Dryden, Pope, Byron—is more

often directed against people than institutions. Satire, I suspect, is usually written by powerless people; it is an act of revenge.

QUERY: And what about *The Oasis?*

MMcC: It's the only one of my books that aimed at the moral reform of its targets. I really think I hoped to show them [the realist faction] how they looked and sounded, with a view to their amendment.

The reception of *The Oasis* was critically excellent, personally trying. Philip Rahv's anger and the rumor that he was thinking of suing Mary McCarthy have already been noted. Another libel suit was instituted by a stranger whose name happened to be identical to one in the book. Editors of *Partisan Review* were unanimously angry. Some persons who were not recognizable in the book but had been involved in the Europe-America Groups were somewhat miffed to be left out of the book. Sidney Hook asked Mary McCarthy: "Why didn't you write about somebody really *big?* The trouble with the book is that those people are all so little. Why don't you pick on somebody really *big?*" The implication seems clear. On the other hand, the historian Hannah Arendt called the book "a gem," and this was the beginning of an enduring friendship between the two women. (The acquaintance had started earlier in the Forties but had been brought to an abrupt stop by an outrageous remark about feeling sorry for Hitler that Mary McCarthy had made toward the end of the war in Hannah Arendt's presence.)

Late in the spring of 1949, and increasingly concerned with anti-Communist politics, an involvement that had been growing steadily more fierce since her early *Partisan Review* days, she and Bowden Broadwater, together with poet Robert

Lowell, critic Elizabeth Hardwick, and Dwight Macdonald, "infiltrated" the Communist-inspired and -backed Peace Conference at the Waldorf Hotel in New York and made fiery anti-Communist speeches from the floor. She remembers that the event was "amusing," and that she wrote a "bad" short story about it which was never published.

In the fall of that year, Broadwater was again "at liberty," having resigned his *Partisan Review* job over a dispute about a salary cut. He was finding it difficult to get another job when Mary McCarthy inherited some money from the McCarthy side of the family. In the face of the fact that "no one was speaking to us anyway since *The Oasis*," the disappointments caused by the progress of the cold war ("the illusion that had preceded *The Oasis* involving the formation of Europe-America Groups had come to nothing"), and the overcrowded Anthill, with Reuel getting bigger, they decided to find a house in Portsmouth, near Newport, Rhode Island, where, it was decided, she would have more time to write. They'd seen Newport the summer before and liked it, so in the winter of 1949 they bought an old house and fixed it up. Reuel came with them and went to St. Michael's School in Newport. This house was to serve as home for more than three years, and while living here, Mary McCarthy gathered together the stories that compose the collection *Cast a Cold Eye*. Published in 1950, it contains a varied group of stories, some of which had appeared first in magazines. Distinguished chiefly by its excellent title, a quotation from the epitaph Yeats wrote for himself ("Cast a cold eye, on life, on death./ Horseman, pass by") which has served a generation of reviewers with a tag to attach to Mary McCarthy's "detached and chilly glance" (and which Robert Lowell tried to persuade her not to use for that very reason), it contains as well two notable stories; two chapters of autobiography that will later turn up again in *Memories of a Catholic Girlhood;* an autobiographical sketch, "C.Y.E.," of no special interest except that it poses the author in a way we grow gradually accustomed to seeing her in her work, as the unsure outsider, a young girl painfully sensitive to what others think and say, made a butt of by the in-group's application to her of a mysterious cognomen; and a poorish story, "The Old Men," which seems contrived, a "setup" circumstance which comes to an ironic but not entirely satisfactory conclusion.

Another story in the collection, "The Weeds," is worth stopping at a moment, although to my mind it too is not a complete success. The trouble lies, I think, in its tone, which is feminine, self-pitying, and sometimes almost foolish. What happens is internal to the mind of the heroine; it is her constant voice, sometimes rising to a whine, that we hear. The events of the story, seen from this private and raw corner of her mind and told in this voice, make the reader suffer with her as she tries to leave her husband, then does, and then is forced by a collapse of will and mentality to go back to him and her weed-filled garden. But then, feeling constricted and without air in the space the author has given him, the reader becomes restless, irritable, impatient and finally physically uncomfortable. He needs to be let out of the locked chamber of the heroine's self-pity and unhappiness.

The woman in this story (never named) is a close relative to Meg Sargent. She too sees herself projected into a series of roles: "And all at once the vision of herself as a young widow slipped into her fancy, like a view into an old stereopticon. She saw herself pale and beautiful in black. . . ." and then "She saw herself, anonymous, in a maid's room in the third story of a house in Pelham. . . ." and "She could see her own case now. . . ." The sight of her real life is always preceded by these visions. Further, she is like another McCarthy heroine who sees marriage as a most imperfect, even horrendous, state, and is in the process, when we meet her, of leaving a husband. Of marriage and its usual consequences, Mary McCarthy writes here: "A marriage made out of loneliness and despair will be lonely and desperate," and "Murder is more civilized than divorce; the Victorians, as usual, were wiser." The heroine, like her corporate relative in *The Company She Keeps,* tends to think in religious terms: "her penitential exercise, her agony in the garden," her husband's attempts "to bring about a resurrection," the oxymoronic reference to "a religious ceremony, a secular Easter Mass." The story is heavy with feelings of inadequacy ("Oh God, oh God, she said to herself, I am unfit—who will hire me?"), of strained nerves and, at times, painfully honest femininity at the merciless hands of a brutal and dishonest man. But the pity of it all, the inequality of the protagonists, spoil the story. Someone has noticed the resemblance of this story to the "sensibility" stories of Katherine Mansfield, has indeed thought it a take-off on them. The resemblance is there, but one doubts that the tone is intended to be satiric.

The two pieces that make the book well worth the reader's time are the Jamesian story, "The Cicerone," and a brilliant piece of essay-writing in the form of a story, "The Friend of the Family." "The Cicerone," first, is a very funny story in journey form; it contains a number of memorable portraits and is, in a sense, a continuation of the form of *The Company She Keeps;* the familiar heroine, now unmarried, is keeping new company. Again the encounters are with the shady, the picturesque and the amoral. And more evidence of Mary McCarthy's evident affection for the revelatory feminine detail is in this story. The young couple through whose eyes the story is told (although it is mainly the young woman's, since Mary McCarthy has stayed close to Meg in voice, and the young man who is her companion is rather shadowy) are traveling together in Europe just after World War II. "Victors in a world war of unparalleled ferocity, heirs of imperialism and the philosophy of the enlightenment, they walked proudly on the dilapidated streets of Europe." Echoes of Henry James are heard in the story (it was an echo the author herself was well aware of and the only influence she has ever acknowledged); the story proceeds along vaguely Jamesian lines. The young couple meet the cicerone, Mr. Sciarappa, on a train. The snobbish young man, based to some extent on Bowden Broadwater, is convinced the cicerone is a bounder. Mr. Sciarappa's age is undeterminate, he moves lightly (even his announced business is symbolic: silk) and mysteriously. In Milan he fastens himself upon them, monopolizing them. In an effort to shake him they tell him about an American heiress now back in Europe after her war exile in America. In Venice, plump, rich, exotic, picturesquely dressed, the heiress Miss Grabbe, perpetually "in pursuit of love," makes love to the cicerone ("matter of factly") and then "thanks him for a very pleasant evening." He leaves precipitously, and occurs again in the lives of the young couple in other Italian cities until, at the last, they run him to ground in a shabby house in Rome. The story is a jewel with two first-rate portraits, the heiress and the cicerone. There is an underlying pursuit theme, in which the young couple seek to know more about the cicerone, and this helps to intensify the effect of half-light revelation. The story is filled with La Rochefoucauld-like epigrams: "The desire to believe the best of people is a prerequisite for intercourse with strangers; suspicion is reserved for friends"; "The three spoke very little together, and it was this that gave them that linked and wedded look"; "What passes for love in our competitive society is frequently envy." Again her use of foreign words and phrases is heavy. A few reviewers and many readers find this tendency of Mary McCarthy's annoying. In this story she confesses to using a foreign word to express "something for which there is no English word" but in later stories, like "The Hounds of Summer" the usage is so pronounced that the audience for the story narrows down to those who can move freely in Italian and French, with a sprinkling of German. She is then writing for a kind of continental, an international culture. Even *The New Yorker* reacted to this exclusiveness by asking her to translate much of the foreign conversation in this story. She did so, but has said she intends to restore it to the original languages when the story is reprinted.

There is, as well, a heavy sprinkling of nineteenth-century turns of phrase, most of them connected with the heart: "Her heart turned over with horror," "her sensibility quivered," "a dreadful presentiment flicked her heart," "how dare you, her heart muttered," "a pain gripped her heart," etc. This retreat to an older diction is like her tendency suddenly to introduce an outrageous image into what is otherwise cool, classical prose. This stirs the reader to attention and warns him not to rely comfortably on modernity of expression, or on the classic regularity he has come to expect.

The story contains a few references to Mary McCarthy's often-repeated theme of humor in sex. We catch a glimpse of Mr. Sciarappa making love to Miss Grabbe, and "tossing the scapular he wore about his neck, and which hung down and interfered with his lovemaking, back again and again, lightly and recklessly over his thin shoulder." Miss Grabbe keeps her blackmarket lira in her douche bag, the kind of detail that will proliferate in *The Group*. The incongruity of these details, one suspects, is intended. Mary McCarthy's honesty will not let her leave out a detail, no matter how seemingly outrageous, unexpected, uncustomary in a work of fiction, if it was *true,* a fact. There are occasional images that are, to my mind, mischosen: "She [Miss Grabbe] was always the second to laugh at a pratfall of her spirit; Mr. Sciarappa, at worst, could only be another banana peel on the vaudeville of her history." Lapses like this, however, are few, and tend to punctuate with shock what is otherwise graceful, free-flowing, detached-sounding prose, immediate and beautifully formed. Finally, it will come as no surprise to those who have come this far to hear that the reliance upon religious imagery is again very noticeable: *"Ita missa est,"* remarks the young lady "sardonically" at one point, and Italian politeness is described as having "a covert sense of performance . . . in which one could trace . . . the half-theatrical swish of the altar-boy's skirts." There are a number of others.

The second story is not a story at all but an essay. One journal, in remarking on Mary McCarthy's stories, said that they "have an air of profound political essays" and this is true of "The Friend of the Family," although here it is not so much political theory she is exploring as a social one. It is a dissertation on marital battle strategy, a subtle yet cruel anatomization of the struggle between men and women for their individual rights. Francis Cleary is the metamorphosing friend who never marries but serves as mediator and neutral party in the war that is marriage. The essay explores such subjects as why one party in a marriage objects to the friends of the other, why persons of one nature choose partners who are totally different from them, the private motives behind the hatred felt after the choice is made, the mediatory role of the Friend of the Family with the children, the dangers inherent in his finding special favor with the children, and so forth. At some points the essay becomes almost Socratic, rhetorical, a question and answer session: "Will the dubious reader acknowledge. . . ?"; "Let anyone . . . ask himself why he does not like his wife's friends."

In the essay war imagery is dominant: "There is another kind of marriage, where it is the partner who is the incidental victim: simply a hostage—whom we have carried home from a raid on the enemy. . . . We bear this person no actual ill will; we may even pity him as we lop off an ear or a little finger in some nicety of reprisal." Winning the war is the point: "There are people who, whatever their good intentions, cannot renounce love, and there are people, a large number, who cannot renounce victory." The war ends in a treaty: "Our lives become a series of disarmament conferences; I will reduce my demands if you will reduce yours with parity as our aim. . . ." Francis Cleary realizes his friendship with the couple is doomed; he will be put out eventually, but if the couple cannot bring this off their only solution is to *become* Francis Cleary themselves because, after all, they are indistinguishable from him.

In the course of the essay there are incisive explorations of the self: "We cannot, in the end, possess anything that is not ourselves, that vivacity, money, respectability, talent which we hoped to add to ourselves by marriage are, we discover to our surprise, unassimilable to our very natures." If it is true that, in this essay-story, as one writer has claimed, "no two people observe each other with tenderness" and that "in her cosmology all are separate" (as if it were very different in the real world) it is even truer that in their separateness they tend to know themselves better and in their incommunicativeness with each other to better communicate their discoveries about themselves and others to the reader. The illusion that human beings communicate, especially in the intimate relationship of marriage, is not Mary McCarthy's. She is a diarist of the separate, whose cure is self-knowledge, not the search for solace from others.

Finally, if the piece is satiric, it is satire at her tenderest. Dudley Fitts says of the story:

> All satire, like all preaching, is autobiography. It may disguise itself . . . or it may seek to hide itself in symbols . . . Yet it is inevitably self-centered, and it is this that accounts for the powerful charm in "The Friend of the Family." Ostensibly fiction, actually so close to confession that it is a relief when Mary McCarthy stops. . . .

The relief comes, not so much when she stops, as when the reader comes to relax in the realization that, like the couple, he too is Francis Cleary. At this point his defensiveness and his sharp critical eye both give way, and he experiences some of the relief of self-recognition.

V *Everything Observed*

"Myself am the groundwork of my book."

—Montaigne, *Essais*

NEW YORK, 1956.

Courtesy of Inge Mörath, Magnum Photos

Courtesy of Inge Mörath, Magnum

WITH KEVIN, LOOKING AT PHOTOGRAPH ALBUM, 1956.

WITH
SHERIDAN,
KEVIN, AND
RESTON, 1958.

Courtesy of
Mary McCarthy

'ITH BOWDEN,
KEVIN, SHERI-
)AN, PRESTON,
THEIR WIVES
AND A FEW
)ESCENDANTS,
1958.

Courtesy of
Mary McCarthy

ABOVE LJUBLJANA, YUGOSLAVIA, 1960.

Courtesy of Mary McCarthy

Courtesy of Mary McCarthy

IN MILAN, 1960.

Courtesy of Mary McCarthy

REUEL AT WEDDING OF MARY McCARTHY TO JAMES WEST, PARIS, 1961.

Courtesy of Mary McCarthy

WITH JAMES WEST IN NANCY, APRIL, 1961.

WITH REUEL IN NANCY, APRIL, 1961.

Courtesy of Mary McCarthy

WITH JANET FLANNER IN PARIS.

STILL living in Newport in 1950 (except for a brief visit to Vassar at *Holiday's* behest to write the article, "The Vassar Girl" and a last visit to her bedridden Grandmother Preston in Seattle, the fictional report of which appears in "Ask Me No Questions" in *Memories of a Catholic Girlhood*) Mary McCarthy had settled down to write *The Groves of Academe.*

The academic novel has a considerable history in the United States. In 1962 *The College Novel in America* by John O. Lyons was devoted to enumerating and evaluating this subgroup of the novel genre. He concluded that nothing really good has been written in the field, although Mary McCarthy's book is one of the few he calls successful. A number of well-known writers have tried to write such novels: Edith Wharton *(The Valley of Decision* in 1902), Nathaniel Hawthorne, who wrote about his student years at Bowdoin in *Fanshawe,* and more recently, May Sarton, Theodore Morrison, James Thurber, T. S. Stribling and so forth. Leslie Fiedler has noted that the sparsity of good college novels (he too in part excepts *The Groves of Academe* as "a witty and satisfying book") is perhaps due to "the incestuous nature of the academic novel." It usually is a book about the writer himself in his role as college professor, and as such has failure as the subject. The author is "too motivated by frustration and impotence originating in the doomed battle between the writer and the Establishment."

The impetus to write the book may have been the result of her short and often frustrating teaching experience at Bard and Sarah Lawrence. Whether or not she was avidly collecting subject matter there, as Randall Jarrell has suggested, is immaterial, but that she *did* find material is evident in *The Groves of Academe*. She is firm in asserting, however, that the scene of the novel is neither college:

> I didn't want to make a composite of those places. I really wanted to make a weird imaginary college of my own. I even took a trip to the Mennonite country in Pennsylvania to try to find a perfect location for it, which I found... somewhere near Ephrata, yes, it was Lititz, Pennsylvania, the home of the pretzel. There's a very charming, old-fashioned sort of academy, a girl's college there.... It had a perfect setting, I thought, for this imaginary college of mine.

Not Sarah Lawrence then ("almost no resemblance to it," she claims), not much of Bard ("a *bit* like Bard"), not Bennington College ("There was not supposed to be anything of Bennington at all," although this was an identification a number of persons tried to make), Jocelyn College, Pennsylvania, is a progressive school containing all the shortcomings and occasional advantages of many such existing places. The college is headed by Maynard Hoar, a president who "like most administrators... was a man who felt himself to be misunderstood and welcomed any opportunity . . . of displaying his broad humanity." A political progressive and yet not an intellectual, Hoar has a history of fearless liberalism, his reputation stemming mainly from the publication in *The American Scholar* of an article, "The Witch Hunt in Our Universities." He is responsible for the hiring of the novel's "monstrous" hero, Henry (often called "Hen") Mulcahy, a repulsive moral child who comes to Jocelyn mainly on the strength of his rumored radical past, and Hoar's reputation as a liberal. "A modern witness to the ordeal by slander," he now stands in the wonderfully ironic position of being safe in a progressive college with a reputation of liberalism to maintain *because* he was once *said* to be a Communist. He has been at Jocelyn two years when the novel begins, with the arrival on his desk of his letter of dismissal from President Hoar. In sly, clever and fascinatingly dishonest fashion, Mulcahy gathers together arguments to compel his being retained on the faculty. He recognizes that the President cannot afford the suspicion that he is being dropped for political reasons, that Hoar could not have it known that he had got rid of an inconvenient critic, and so he compounds the confusion of motives and lies by suggesting to the faculty that his wife is dangerously ill and that word of his dismissal might well kill her. In contrast to Mulcahy's deviousness is Maynard Hoar's decent administrative behavior; even his looks serve this contrast. "He was one of those rugged men who looked exactly like their photographs—dark, resilient, keen-eyed, buoyant, yet thoughtful. Like all such official types he specialized in being his own antithesis: strong but understanding, boisterous but grave, pragmatic but speculative when need be." Then look at Mulcahy:

> A tall, soft-bellied, lisping man with a tense, mushroom-white face, rimless bifocals, and greying thin red hair, he was

> intermittently aware of a quality of personal unattractiveness that emanated from him like a miasma; this made him self-pitying, uxorious, and addicted also to self-love. . . . The unwholesome whiteness of his long, pear-shaped body, the droop of his trousers, his children's runny noses and damp bottoms, his wife's woman's complaint, the sand sprinkling the lashes of his nearsighted, glaucous eyes. . . .

To his support, Mulcahy, who seems to compel support *because* of the appeal of his "heretical flavor" to the middle-class "progressive community," rallies a number of faculty members of goodwill. He then successfully presents to them his multifabricated case, composed of his phony Communist past, his suggested anti-Communist present, and his wife Cathy's health which, he contends, the President is callously ignoring in firing him. Never for a moment does he face, or allow his sympathizers to face for long, the possibility that he is being let go for perfectly justifiable, academic reasons. Only the head of his department, Howard Furness, a realist who considered "all attainment, idealism, and so forth, to be a sort of speciousness," has no sympathy for Hen and refuses to join the defense party. Eventually the defense prevails. Impressed by faculty support, the President reappoints him. But by this time, disillusion has set in among his more fervent followers, who have discovered that in a number of matters crucial to his case he has lied. Following a wonderfully entertaining Poets' Conference held in spring on the campus—one of the high points of the novel, although Mary McCarthy, with her usual hypercritical approach to her own work, thinks it poorly done, and that it "could have been much better"—it becomes clear that Mulcahy never *was* a Communist and has no real "heretical past." At the Conference, The Poet of the Masses, another McCarthy Irishman, seems to be greeting Mulcahy as a former comrade, but upon questioning by the President and Furness, reveals that this suggested party membership was not so. The poet, feeling guilty at having allowed himself to be questioned, tells Mulcahy about it. Now Hen is in a position to victimize the President. Delighted, he in turn threatens to expose Hoar's antiliberalist, Joe-McCarthy-like act, and thus to ruin his liberal reputation. So the novel comes to its wickedly paradoxical conclusion. The President, who had fired Mulcahy for legitimate reasons and then rehired him against his better judgment, *himself* resigns, with an explanation that is both deeply sincere and metaphorically mixed. "I saw that I was too much incriminated. The college would never get rid of him as long as I was at the tiller. With another skipper who can't be blackmailed there's a fair chance of getting him out." As James Yaffe has said: "It is a neat and clever inversion of the situation in the usual liberal novel of college life in which the highly successful liberal teacher is dismissed for leftist ideas."

The novel is a virtuoso attack on a number of shibboleths. The major one is, of course, the progressive educational system. The old poet asks: "Is this the fabled college where everything is run backwards?" The reply is indeed no, "the courses ran normally from the immediate past to the present." Further, the element of fantasy is strong at Jocelyn, "the freakish character of its tides of opinion, the anomalies of its personnel, the madness of its methodology which had produced here a world like a child's idea of China, with everything upside down."

A second, and by now well-known, target is liberalism. Of Domna Rejnev, twenty-three-year-old Russian instructor from Radcliffe and would-be revolutionary, it is said, "at bottom she was conventional, believing in a conventional moral order and shocked by deviations from it into a sense of helpless guilt toward the deviator. In other words she was a true liberal." A third point of attack is the faculty, in particular and as a class. Of one of them, Van Tour, she says, "Like many teachers of English he was not able to think clearly." The intellectual faculty holds tight to the usual progressive-college field period for students, not in any sense for the students' edification, but to preserve their own vacations. They are the ones to benefit most from the foolish freedom given their students who are "too disorderly or lazy or ill-trained to carry anything very far without the spur of discipline." Another, equally vulnerable target is the student: the cataloguing of their types and the easy predictability of their futures provide some of the best reading in the novel.

Women, as is usual in Mary McCarthy's books, come out somewhat better than the men, but they too do not go unscathed. Alma Fortune at one point intercedes between Domna and Furness: " 'No need to quarrel,' she said tersely and the room came to order. Her voice was like a pointer moving sharply on a map or blackboard, which gave her an air of authoritative impersonality, though as a matter of fact she was congenitally nervous and suffered from intermittent eczema, asthma, shingles, and all the usual disorders of the repressed female brain-worker." Characteristically, when Mary McCarthy attacks, it is in the familiar form of the hardly defensible generalization: "Like most European women when they argue, she was both angry and zestful." She takes oblique aim at the pretensions of the critic-teacher too, by suggesting the self-identification of Irish-Catholic Mulcahy to James Joyce: "As a prophet of modern literature in a series of halfway-good colleges, he had gladly accepted an identification with the sacred untouchables of the modern martyrology—with Joyce, the obscure language teacher...

He carried an ashplant in imitation of Joyce's Stephen Dedalus. . . ."

Here Mary McCarthy's penchant for religious imagery is most apparent. More than one amateur student of the novel has attempted an identification between Mulcahy and Christ, an identification Mulcahy himself tends to make. A chapter is called *Mea Culpa;* Hen's reference to the Mystical Body ("We are members, one of another"); Pilate's speech, echoed to the President: "Have nothing to do, Maynard, with this just man."); Henry's reference to his dismissal (*"Ita missa est"*); and the description of the rest of the faculty in relation to him, "like so many gingerly Thomases who content themselves with fingering the wounds he held out to them and attesting to their intellectual superiority by their readiness to believe the incredible." Henry's ice-cream container is "a chalice," he is defined by John Bentkoop as a "victim, one who must be more concerned about himself than anybody else is for him. Even Christ on the cross had such a moment: 'My God, My God, why hast thou forsaken me?' " There are other such similarities, more the result of Mary McCarthy's "great compulsion, really a dreadful compulsion," as she has said, "to make these references," than of any attempt to make the monstrous Henry Mulcahy a Christ figure, except as, in her voice speaking through Mulcahy in another of his complexities, he tends to think this way himself. She has said, when an interviewer pointed out her more-than-ordinary use of religious imagery: "I think I do it as a sort of secret signal, a sort of looking over the heads of the readers who don't recognize them to the readers who do understand them." Asked if they are *only* literary and therefore blasphemous, she says: "They are secret jokes, they *are* blasphemies. But I think that religion offers to Americans very often the only history and philosophy they ever get. A reference to it somehow opens up that historical vista. In that sense it is a device for deepening the passage."

It is safe to say that Mary McCarthy has been incapable of writing at any length without resorting to such imagery. (Only in *The Group* does it finally disappear as a stylistic characteristic.) Henry's sense of himself, half-Joycean martyr, half-Christ (he has been raised a Catholic, like his author), is partly the result of, and partly the cause of, the usage she has called obsession. Domna sees the literary-Christian identification, "Henry Mulcahy is Christ in the disguise of Bloom and Earwicker, the family men, the fathers eternal consubstantial with the Son," and John Bentkoop adds, "Christ's experience is the great paradigm for the persecution psychosis." Thus the novel and the portrait of Mulcahy become much more complex than at first sight, marvelously subtle, and the suggested madness of Mulcahy adds another line of possibility. Domna says, "I think Henry is mad. He has a delusional system centering on Joyce. He speaks of Joyce's life as a Ministry. . . . He believes that he's been subject to persecution for propagating the Word. . . . He is hated by Joyce's enemies, who comprise the whole academic world. . . . His Communist period was a ritual conversion symbolizing Joyce's baptism in the religion of naturalism—the precursor. And the Communists hate him because he transcended naturalism, just as they hate Joyce."

Mulcahy joins that cadre of literary figures who have confused themselves with literary figures, real or imagined, somewhat in the manner of Madame Bovary, Tom Sawyer, Dumas' Camille, William Dean Howells' Editha and Penelope Lapham and others, all misled, dazed, by the same error in identity. Domna too wonders, "What would Tolstoy say?" to solve a moral dilemma at one point. Walking consciously in the footsteps of literary models is one trouble with Henry; another, as John Lyons has suggested, is that he has been corrupted "by the vagaries of modern liberal causes." His is an academic mind, liberal in cast, which does not know how to handle freedom. Like the others, he is an opportunist thriving because the atmosphere allows him the freedom to be false. The gap between his illusions and pretensions about himself, between his motives and his real character, is vast. Only the Poet of the Masses is able to stay free of the academic disease that Mary McCarthy has diagnosed so bleakly:

> Within twenty hours, he perceived, they had succeeded in leading him up the garden path into one of their academic mazes, where a man could wander for eternity, meeting himself in mirrors. *No,* he repeated. Possibly they were all very nice, high-minded, scrupulous people with only an occupational tendency toward backbiting and a nervous habit of self-correction, always emending, penciling, erasing; but he did not care to catch the bug, which seemed to be endemic in these ivied haunts.

Henry's "Voice" is heard on both the academic and intellectual level and, to make it even more believable, on the personal level as well. His sordid, lower middleclass family life is seen with horrifying reality—his children clutching the crotches of their snowsuits, their sticky hands, his worn-out old car, unpaid bills, the leaky roof of his house, "the ammonia-smell of urine in the back rooms [of his house] owing to the pads drying out on the radiators." If the academic novel often brings with it a good deal of high, allusive shoptalk, it also ought to have its roots in this kind of comic reality. Mary McCarthy saw this in 1948 when, reviewing a play on academic life by John van Druten (*The Druid Circle*), she said that it would have been better "if it had remained on the plane of the ordinary, where the teacher's tragi-comedy really takes place."

The achievement in the creation of the character of Henry Mulcahy is this Voice of the protagonist. Some critics have missed this, and have failed to recognize that it is not Mary McCarthy speaking critically throughout the work but Henry speaking of and through himself. She has managed, for the most part, this difficult physical ventriloquism of putting herself behind the skin of an offensive male anti-hero. When Henry is not present, the Voices become those of other faculty members, or of the President. Their speech is in the main *about* Henry and his problems, his situation, so that in this sense it is an overtone of his own voice, or a reaction to it, like a reversed echo. Only occasionally, in the Poet of the Masses, who wants out of the whole mess, or again, in some of the statements of Domna, with her almost pathological insistence on the truth and her reaction of physical recoil from the lie, is the McCarthy voice heard. This effective dominant Voice was a matter of her hard-fought decision. She notes in "Characters in Fiction" that modern writers are attracted to the technique of writing from the inside of a character totally unlike their own. Of *The Groves of Academe,* she says:

> The normal way of telling this story would be from the outside or from the point of view of one of the professor's sympathizers. But I found I had no interest in telling it that way; to me, the interest lay in trying to see it from the professor's point of view and mouthing it in the clichés and the hissing jargon of his vocabulary. That is, I wanted to know just how it felt to be raging inside the skin of a Henry Mulcahy and to learn how, among other things, he arrived at a sense of self-justification and triumphant injury that allowed him . . . to use any means to promote his personal cause. . . . I had to use every bit of Mulcahy that was in me, and there was not very much . . . I wanted to tiptoe into the interior of Mulcahy like a peasant coming into a palace.

And she ends by saying, "There is an element of the private game, even of the private joke, in this kind of writing —a secret and comic relation between the author and his characters."

The old debate about the nature and the value of her satire is carried on in the reviews of *The Groves of Academe* as in those of her first two books. Robert Halsband in *Saturday Review* said that her understanding of her characters was so successful "that her compassion for them is implicit." In another place he speaks of her "pitiless humility." Robert E. Fitch, on the other hand, finds no compassion; instead he accuses her of pride, of being a traitor to her intellectual class. "She turns her ridicule against the rituals, the tabus, and the credulities of the intelligentsia." Her satire, he says, has the "cerebro-genital emphasis," is "intelligence without tenderness, without humility," and is "relentless, predatory, imperialistic, and without compassion." He is indignant about the absence in her work of "a profound moral passion" which must be present, he insists, in great satire even if, as in Swift, it is "intelligence without tenderness." He implies that, like Alma Fortune, Mary McCarthy "lovingly impaled a moral weakness and squeezed it like a pimple." On the other hand Alice Morris found that the reader regarded Mulcahy with "a sneaking if ill-founded compassion." Joseph Wood Krutch admires her avant-gardism in attacking intellectual orthodoxies when no one else at the moment was doing it. "It's the business of the satirist to be a little ahead of the game." And Richard Hughes is sure that compassion would *spoil* her work. "To ask for sweetness, for compassion, is to misread her fundamental intention. No wash of comfortable sentiment will ever blur her incorruptible vision because for her, commitment would ultimately involve compromise."

Once again her satire is attacked because it is directed against her friends. Isaac Rosenfeld in *The New Republic* goes further and says that "it cannot be successful satire—it is too dependent on the object of its own ridicule, it derives from and always returns to the institutions it would like to destroy. And what satire fails in its attempts to destroy, it tends to strengthen and preserve." His claim is that Mary McCarthy satirizes in order "to break her dependence" on "a world of ridiculous objects" to which she herself belongs. This runs parallel to Brendan Gill's theory that "her standards of conduct are so high that . . . we despair of matching them, and we sense her despair of matching them."

The fact that she uses what she herself is, the group of which she is a member, the persons who are fellow members, the old ideals in which she once put her trust, as the objects of her satire for therapeutic reasons ("self-castigation" is another accusation) is of course one of those statements that cannot be denied or defended. It would seem that satire directed from the inside works better than from a distance, is more informed and more likely to be based upon fact and to elicit from the writer the same fury he felt in the original, real-life situation, just as utilizing real persons creates a kind of stamp of actuality for the character. Incidentally, it should be noted that, although (according to Mary McCarthy) *The Groves of Academe* is "full of real people," and Henry Mulcahy was based on one real person she had known ("*not* an Irishman," she says), few critics attacked her for having written a cruel *roman à clef,* as in the case of "Portrait of the Intellectual as a Yale Man" in *The Company She Keeps* and *The Oasis.* The reason is probably ignorance; she was here operating in an area where the literary critics were not likely to be familiar with the originals, so the identifications did not bother them at all.

And then, as is inevitable with Mary McCarthy's novels, one comes after all to questions of style. In addition to the wealth of religious imagery in the book, it is equally rich in classical allusions, beginning of course with its title. Cadmus, Alcibiades, Draco, Sulla and Diocletian, Plato, Calliope, Hermes and Olympus, Galatea all are used as image or allusion in the book, and this profusion of Attic echoes contributes to the effectiveness of the academic subject matter. One chapter title, "Lucubrations," draws upon its original Greek meaning, "night-thoughts," a witty classical reference for the evening meeting of the English department. This amount of classical reference reminds one of the author's preference for the "old-fashioned, classical" disciplines, the traditional education that Miss Sandison and Vassar represent to her over the progressive *laissez-faire* of Jocelyn, the approach which, conservative that she is in such matters, she instinctively distrusts.

This novel provides added evidence that Mary McCarthy's fiction is very close to the spirit of the essay. It is a novel of ideas with a number of amusing characters to promulgate them. They come together in the by-now familiar McCarthy community, an intellectual gathering from which "she dispatches her characters out on perilous voyages, weighing them down with the accumulated intellectual baggage of the overburdened contemporary liberal," as Riley Hughes has put it. Whole sections of the novel are pure exposition, of the college's philosophy, of its curriculum, of the intricate and almost symbolic relationships among the faculty and between faculty and students, the economics of higher education, etc. What Riley Hughes labeled "the brilliant movement of ideas in action" is in truth a kind of essay with fictional trimmings on the illiberalities of liberalism, the vagaries and misuses of academic freedom by the academic, the contradictions involved in orthodoxies which once were heresies, and so forth. From *The Groves of Academe* we remember one major comic portrait, Mulcahy, the unavoidable sound of his unpleasant Voice pursuing us down the corridors of his nasty mind, and a number of well-documented and well-illustrated theses.

* * *

By 1952 Mary McCarthy and Bowden Broadwater had become increasingly restless in Portsmouth. "The land across the way that we thought was a rich man's pasture turned out to belong to a Portuguese who sold it all off in lots—with hideous little houses in rows—and we couldn't bear that. Then I began to go away quite a bit, which I ascribe to Bowden's being restless, perhaps." Politics was part of the cause of her restlessness, as well as the failure to get on with the novel she had begun, *The Group*. She had started it that fall and had got as far as the third chapter, the scene where Dottie sits disconsolately on a bench in Washington Square Park. She found she could not continue:

> I thought it was just so terrible, so sad and I felt, these poor girls. . . . It was going to be a kind of mock chronicle novel, going from the inauguration of Roosevelt to the inauguration of Eisenhower. And I felt that I was punishing, cruel to those poor girls whose lives, whose futures looked worse. . . . When I broke off—it would have been 1933—things were already so terrible at that point that I stopped.

As for politics, after the disheartening defeat of Adlai Stevenson, a campaign in which she was not actively but only emotionally involved, and her horror at the McCarthy hearings in Washington, she began to think that she herself might be a force in civil rights questions. "I was terribly worked up about the constitutional aspects of the McCarthy business and it seemed that the judiciary—not even the lawyers really—were the only ones who stood firm." She thought of getting a law degree. To an interviewer she later told the story:

> I conceived the ridiculous idea of going to Harvard Law School. I was all set to take the tests—but really, I was too old to absorb the material. . . . I finally called an old friend, Judge Biggs of the Pennsylvania Court of Appeals, and he told me, don't do anything until I'd talked to him. So he came down with his wife in his white Jaguar for a weekend, and he talked me out of it.

Further symptom of her growing personal restlessness, as well as her discontent with the American political climate and the press and magazines that represented it, was her idea, after the Law School dream fell through, of starting a new magazine with friends, Dwight Macdonald, Richard Rovere, Arthur Schlesinger, Jr., and Hannah Arendt. She was to be the editor, the magazine was, in the main, her idea; its title was to be *Critic* ("a terrible name," she later said). Conceived as a middle-of-the-road publication, not as far left as Macdonald's *Politics* and not as far right as the existing Democratic organs, the idea came to nothing, collapsing on the rocks of finance. She was able to raise only about half of the hundred thousand dollars the magazine needed. Brock Brower, in an article entitled "Mary McCarthyism," sees the progress of these idealistic dreams as typical of what happens in her novels. "It is so very much the sort of thing —the Intellectual Fray, the Exploded Hope, the Niggardliness of Political Virtue, the Hypocrisy of Commitment— upon which her own literary imagination turns."

Disappointed at this failure, she was honest about her own

motives, and in her analysis of the reasons for it: "On the one hand I have a desire to be an activist, and on the other, I don't." During this time, too, she renewed or recovered her friendship with Philip Rahv: she had invited him to be a member of *Critic*'s editorial board.

Her restlessness, and Bowden Broadwater's, made them decide to sell the Portsmouth house. In the fall of that year, during a visit to the Cape, they had seen another house they liked. Upon the sale of the Portsmouth place they bought it; this is the controversial place in Wellfleet not too far from where Edmund Wilson now lived with his new wife and child. The Broadwaters spent the winter before they moved into the new house in New York at the Hotel Chelsea.

In 1953, having given up the writing of *The Group,* Law School, and *Critic,* Mary McCarthy had run out of money. She, Bowden Broadwater, and Reuel (for her part of his vacation) summered in East Montpelier, Vermont, the scene of the events that appear in the short story "The Appalachian Revolution." They did not go to their house in Wellfleet because she and Edmund Wilson had agreed that the Broadwaters would not be there while Reuel was staying with Edmund Wilson. In the fall, however, they *did* go back to their new house, with all the accompanying doubts about the rectitude of returning that she has described in *A Charmed Life,* and there she began that novel, conceived first as a short story. In the next year, in Portugal (where she did a long travel piece for *The New Yorker,* "Letter from Portugal") she went on with the novel, and in Capri, early in 1955, she finished it.

I have already discussed the autobiographical elements in this novel, the divergent views of the portrait of Miles Murphy as Edmund Wilson, and the clear identification of the initial situation of the novel—the return of the young couple to New Leeds while her former husband is still living there with his family—with the Broadwaters' return to Wellfleet. There are more. Martha Sinnott bears a close resemblance to her creator, whose great-grandmother's given name she bears. Martha is an "artist" (an ex-actress and playwright, just as the mother of the hero of the novel she is now working on is a famous harpsichordist), and somehow not entirely unlike Mary McCarthy in some details: "a strange poetical-looking being with very fair, straight hair done in a little knot, a quaint oval face with very dark, wide-set eyes, and a small, slight figure. . . ." (Mary McCarthy, seeing no resemblance whatever, has said that Martha is modeled after a girl she knew in her youth.) It is said of Martha that she "was exaggerating or that she was very clever, which amounted to the same thing." Martha spoke only the literal truth—"that was her peculiarity." Besides her very noticeable honesty, she has "clarity of mind . . . she has a sharp ear and a lively natural style," she is extraordinarily acute at noticing things ("she was very feminine that way") and is capable of full self-knowledge. As she debates the prospect of an abortion (for the main plot, which is in no respect autobiographical, of *A Charmed Life* revolves around a drunken sexual reunion that Martha has with Miles, her first husband, during her second husband's absence, after which she becomes pregnant, with no way of knowing whose child she is bearing), her ethical nature is explored:

> Yet all the while the moral part of Martha knew that she would have to have an abortion because all her inclinations were the other way. The hardest course was the right one; in her experience, this was an almost invariable law. If her nature shrank from the task, if it hid and cried piteously for mercy, that was a sign that she was in the presence of the ethical.

The search for Voice goes on in *A Charmed Life*. The author seems to assure us that the Voice heard is Martha's and is not hers. In "Characters in Fiction" she says:

> These books [*A Charmed Life* and *The Groves of Academe*] are impersonations, ventriloquial acts; the author, like some prankster on the telephone, is speaking in an assumed voice —high or deep, hollow or falsetto, but in any case, not his own.

If Martha Sinnott is not the author, the reader can only know this by a separate assertion of the author; all evidence, it seems, points to an identification, and it would be hard to prove her point. Later she explained that she was talking about Miles' voice as an act of ventriloquism in the essay and acknowledged that "Martha's voice *is* mine." This is not true, of course, of the Voice in *The Groves of Academe,* where the evidence for ventriloquism is all in her favor.

If Martha is Mary, one may assume that the rather stuffy husband John Sinnott is, essentially, Bowden Broadwater, but that is not entirely true, she insists, except for a small part of him. She thinks the character in the novel is very weak because, being neither Bowden nor entirely "a young friend of ours" on whom he is partially based, he comes out a very vague character. The character Sinnott got his name because Mary McCarthy saw the name in a newspaper and its apparent composition (Sin-Not) appealed to her. She was not aware that the name is an Irish one, and that by naming John this she was adding to her string of Irish heroes. When she found out she was "horrified. I had not intended him to be Irish at all."

The other characters in *A Charmed Life* are a group of bohemians living past the summer season into a Cape Cod winter. ("The inhabitants," says John to Martha when they are talking about going to New Leeds, "from your own account, seem to bear a charmed life.") There is the artist and his wife, Warren and Jane Coe, based so closely on real originals that "the original of Warren, after the publication of the novel, was struck dumb for some time. He was unable to ask his usual questions or say things like, 'Pardon my French.' This left him without conversation." There is a Frenchman who dabbles in everything from the Roman Catholic Church to antiques to the sale of liquor to Alcoholics Anonymous, a vicomte with "a rich air of fraudulence," who belongs to the little circle of likable, colorful frauds in Mary McCarthy's fiction. There is the virginal young woman artist, Dolly Lamb (a version of Dottie in *The Group*), and her Australian art-critic and former-Communist friend who has "something Christ-like about his appearance," who is suing for the return of his children from this third wife after his fourth wife has left him. All the winter residents in the group are artists, in some way involved with one another. This gives the novel the customary McCarthy air of a laboratory experiment. She seems to be saying to the reader: let us see how things will work out when these people are all put together in one place with all their absurd pretensions to intellectualism or creativity.

How they work out is simple: they either, in the manner of all comic characters, remain precisely as they were when we first met them—this is true of the essentially comic Miles (his behavior in the seduction scene on the slippery sofa in Martha's living room is further testimony to the ludicrous nature of the sex act), of the Coes, of John Sinnott, the vicomte, of Sandy and Dolly. Only to Martha does anything really happen so that she "comes along" as a character. She is able to view herself pitilessly and to understand the real problem for her, the customary ambiguity involved in making a moral choice. Mary McCarthy has noted earlier this phenomenon, in "Yellowstone Park": "I felt caught in a dilemma that was new to me then but which since has become horribly familiar: the trap of adult life in which you are held, wriggling, powerless to act because you can see both sides." In *A Charmed Life* she adds: "We act as if the human race had learned nothing... as soon as we think something it occurs to us that the opposite or the contrary might be true. And no one cares." Martha decides upon an abortion because she cannot bear the dishonesty of not knowing for certain whose child she is carrying. She is on her way to Boston to have the abortion when she is killed instantly in an automobile accident. Mary McCarthy cannot resist the irony (and this was true of the ending of *The Groves of Academe* as well) of the final accident: Martha dies at the precise moment that she realizes she has changed. "She was no longer afraid of herself." At that moment the charmed life of the bohemian intellectual in which she has been preserved is exploded:

> *"Integer vitae, scelerisque purus,"* she sang, thinking of Warren.... Martha slowed down and hugged her own side of the road. As the car crashed into her and she heard a shower of glass, she knew, in a wild flash of humor, that she had made a fatal mistake: in New Leeds, after sundown, she would have been safer on the wrong side of the road.

The last flash of irony, accompanied by a good Latin sentence, is a familiar coda for McCarthy fiction. There are other recognizable McCarthy usages in *A Charmed Life*. To match the Poets' Conference in *The Groves of Academe,* there is a self-contained little nugget of a scene dropped into the book, it would seem, for its own sake; the only apparent connection to the rest of the plot is that it precedes the seduction scene. It is logical but not necessary, a parody of intellectual get-togethers, a reading of Racine's *Bérénice*. Here all of Mary McCarthy's powers of psychological observation, her way of pinning down moral and intellectual weaknesses and then revealing them in flashes of wit, are wonderfully combined.

Critical response to the book was, as it usually is to her work, divided. Most critics found it the least of her books, although Richard Ohmann called it "the best of her novels." Some found it static like *The Oasis:* "She fails to engage her people in any meaningful action." Others felt it was meager in ideas, even though it was possible to see that she was talking in part about the dangers of living among intellectuals who are as well dilettantes and bohemians. Later and looking back, some were to see *A Charmed Life* as an early archetype of *The Group,* with Dolly a progenitor of Dottie Renfrew, and the seduction scene a preparation for the Dottie-Dick section of *The Group.* (It is amusing that *The Library Journal* found *A Charmed Life* "a bit too obstetrical for small libraries," but went on bravely "to recommend it to others.") The idea of lack of progress in contemporary middle-class intellectual (or educated) society is here put forth strongly, to be taken up again nine years later in *The Group.* She is accused, further, of not moving her readers, of being "uncommitted" and "detached." She is credited with doing a bloody vivisection and "sniggering at the act of conception." The *Time* critic spotted (among some flagrant misconceptions) what is clearly a partial truth about *A Charmed Life* and her other fiction, that it contains "cadenced self-recriminations," an insight that calls to mind Simone de Beauvoir's remark that "in one way or another every book is an appeal for help." If Mary McCarthy is not sometimes calling for help, or at times asking for understanding for her personal plight, she is at least recording in fiction her painful, inexorable awareness of the damage that insight does to a vision of oneself, to living in a social group or with political ideas in which one has come to see the flaws. She realizes that the most highly touted moral perceptions are replete with self-delusion.

A Charmed Life was finished in Capri, where Bowden Broadwater and Mary McCarthy were staying in a borrowed villa, in February of 1955. During these months they decided (or more accurately, it was his view) that it had become impossible, after the publication of *A Charmed Life,* to go back to Wellfleet to live. The only thing to do was to sell their Cape Cod house. At Capri, too, there occurred the first really serious altercation between them, the precise cause for which Mary McCarthy contends was "a mystery to me." For a time and despite a reconciliation, they continued to be "on very poor terms." This year was spent in Europe—in Greece, in Paris, the Midi, Saint Tropez. At summer's end Bowden Broadwater and Reuel returned to New York, he to become a teacher at St. Bernard's School. Later he was made assistant headmaster, running the administrative side of the boys' private school that Reuel had attended. Hard as it may be to picture Mary McCarthy as a headmaster's wife, she recalls being much more concerned about the amenities of her situation than her husband. She says that "he was very protective about me" and required of her no official entertaining whatever. Mary McCarthy stayed on in Europe until December to do the research for the book on Venice she had been commissioned to do. In May and through the summer of 1956 she was back in Italy, still working on *Venice Observed,* and Bowden and Reuel joined her in the summer. This was to be the pattern of the next few years: some periods alone in Europe, later in Florence at work at a second travel-art-history and historical critical volume, *The Stones of Florence,* and then summer reunions.

During this time their relationship teetered, she had a love affair which they somehow managed to surmount, and in 1959, still together, they spent the winter in New York, the summer in their old house in Vermont. There, on Bowden's urging, she went back to working on the novel she had abandoned in 1952. It was, apparently, still giving her trouble. To work better she went alone to Tripoli to stay for six weeks with a wealthy woman friend who had a villa there. Under "almost ideal conditions" she turned out prose "like the miller's daughter in Rumpelstiltskin."

Leaving Tripoli at the end of the year, and putting the recalcitrant novel down again, Mary McCarthy was off on a trip to Poland, Yugoslavia, London, and the English universities at the behest of the State Department. She had been asked to give a series of "talks," not written speeches, to audiences in all these places, ranging from university classes to gatherings of young people or senior citizens. "You didn't know what kind of audience you were going to get, so it was useless to prepare. Sometimes you'd find old people in Adult Education, sometimes school children, and you'd just have to improvise to the situation. You know, tell the story of your life, or *anything*."

Out of these talks came Mary McCarthy's two major essays in literary criticism, "The Fact in Fiction," and "Characters in Fiction," as well as the piece "The American Realist Playwrights," which, once it appeared in print, established her reputation for a new generation (since the cutting job she had done on the theatre for *Partisan Review* back in the late Thirties and early Forties) as a wrecker of her literary contemporaries. The three essays, built around the spoken germs of her talks, and in the company of other previously uncollected pieces of journalism and reviews dating back to 1946, constitute the volume of essays, *On The Contrary,* which appeared in the fall of 1961.

The two literary essays are interesting and valuable contributions to the critical literature of the novel, but they are as well important to an understanding of her own fiction. They attempt to establish signposts by which great fiction can be recognized. "The Fact in Fiction" asserts that:

(1) the distinctive mark of the novel is its concern with the actual world, the world of fact, of the verifiable. This passion for facts is a "splendid sickness" which afflicted Austen, Dickens, Balzac, Tolstoi, Dostoievski, Melville, the Joyce of *Ulysses,* Faulkner, etc. All share a deep love of fact, of the empirical element in experience. "The passion for fact in a raw state is a peculiarity of the novel," and the fact in its raw state is the boilerplate of the novel.

(2) the novel is what its name suggests: news, a piece of eyewitness journalism; it is significant that Defoe (author of *The Journal of the Plague Year)* should be regarded as the father of the modern novel.

(3) the novel, to be important, must have an "air of veracity." We must believe it to be "continuous with real life, made of the same stuff." "This love of truth, ordinary common truth recognizable to everyone, is the ruling passion of the novel." And "even when it is most serious, the novel's characteristic tone is one of gossip and tittle-tattle. . . . If the breath of scandal has not touched it, the book is not a novel."

All of this, she points out, raises some difficulties for the contemporary novelist to whom the expanding universe is so overwhelming that the insignificant "finite world of the novelist" seems somehow small and embarrassingly limited. The novel may be dying because it has thus far avoided any encounter with the very real, very gross truths of recent human history—Hiroshima, Buchenwald, etc.—and because, in the face of these unbelievable horrors of the real world, belief in the fictional world must suffer.

"Characters in Fiction," the second essay, goes on to say that:

(1) The modern novel has a lack of great characters. It has been claimed that "there are no *people* any more" in American life because of the disease of conformity, but this is not so much the cause of the loss of character in fiction as the disappearance of "a sense of character" in the novel which began to fade with D. H. Lawrence. There *are* people, but the modern novelist has ceased to describe them.

(2) Having lost their interest in the social, in the novels of sensibility and sensation, and in the recent objective novel in which the very notion of character is ruled out, the novelists (including herself) can no longer "go straight" as Tolstoy did. "We are conscious of being twisted when we write." Further, "much of modern literature might be defined as the search for one's own diametrical opposite which is then used as the point of view." Joyce, the great modern mimic in his interior monologues, may have found "a curious back door" to the concept of character.

(3) Characters in fiction are what they *do,* and ultimately, real characters are comic ones (Mr. Darcy, Mr. Micawber, Falstaff, Molly Bloom, M. Homais) who possess "implacable resistance to change"; "The comic element is the incorrigible element in every human being; the capacity to learn, from experience or instruction, is what is forbidden to all comic creations. . . ." The modern novel has lost both its sense of characters (heroes), its element of suspense and finally, "the power of the author to speak in his own voice." It has failed to explore "the common world that lies between the contemporary reader and the contemporary author."

To take careful note of these comments on the world of

modern fiction is to walk, almost directly, into the novel that is illuminated by these insights and recognitions, *The Group.*

* * *

After her barnstorming lecture tour, the marriage to Bowden Broadwater was over. In Warsaw Mary McCarthy had met James West, who was stationed there as a State Department official. West was married (to his second wife) and had three children. At the end of her lecture tour, Mary McCarthy went to Rome to wait for a divorce. During that year and while staying for a short time in Warsaw, she began again to work on *The Group,* her personal life being so confused at the time that it was a move of pure desperation: "I *had* to do something." Early in 1961, Bowden Broadwater agreed to a divorce, Mary McCarthy flew to the United States, and the divorce was obtained in Alabama in February of that year. In April, Mary McCarthy married James West in Paris.

The consequences of the termination of her third marriage are still not known, for it is said, on good authority, that Broadwater, not remarried, living in New York and administering at St. Bernard's, may be engaged in writing a novel in which Mary McCarthy figures prominently.

Her fourth husband is an extraordinarily handsome and charming man whose looks are reminiscent of her father's. Of this she says, "none of my husbands was good-looking. Of course I've had affairs with good-looking men, but I've never married one—until now." Immediately after their marriage, James West returned to his post in Warsaw, and Mary McCarthy joined him there somewhat later, having managed to cripple herself by slipping a disc in her back in Vienna. Three weeks in a Viennese hospital did very little for her condition; when finally it was possible to join James West in Warsaw, she did so, arriving in a wheelchair. There she was treated by a Polish physician and cured.

Elements of humor marked the start of this fourth marriage. Both James West and Mary McCarthy came to it with almost no possessions. In a novel she is now working on she places her heroine, Rosamund Brown, in a similar "noble" position, although her son Peter "disapproved of her habit of leaving their possessions behind whenever she got a divorce. . . Rosamund claimed that you had to pay for freedom by being willing to give up everything. It was ignoble to latch on to property." Mary McCarthy herself came out of her third divorce with a few books and her mother's silver, West with *his* mother's silver. Later, when they went to England to buy furniture for their Paris apartment, a young man who was showing them London's auction houses suddenly turned to them, taking in their age, and said: "What happened to you people—a *fire?*"

In the fall of 1961 the two went back to the United States on leave from West's post. Mary McCarthy had continued to work on *The Group,* and at this point West was assigned to Paris. In March they returned to Europe. West's new assignment was to the Organization for Economic Cooperation and Development, where he has been stationed since 1962. After a summer in Italy, at Bocca di Magra, which Mary McCarthy has used as setting for the story "The Hounds of Summer,"they settled down into an apartment they had bought on the rue de Rennes, and, at long last, she finished *The Group.* It was published in 1963, and from that moment she was no longer a coterie writer. Her public life as a writer had begun.

VI *The Old Bunch*

DOROTHY: *I'm bored, darling.*

PRESTON: *Don't be a bored Vassar bitch.*

DOROTHY: *Don't call me names, please. I don't feel up to it just now. And besides I'm not typical Vassar. I don't understand* anything *they taught me there.*

PHILIP: *I wouldn't take you.*

DOROTHY: *Why not?*

PHILIP: *Because you're useless, really. You're uneducated, you're useless, you're a fool and you're lazy.*

—Ernest Hemingway: *The Fifth Column*

THE Vassar prototype—or the Seven Sister figure, because to the public mind there is not too much difference between the Vassar girl, the Bryn Mawr girl, the Wellesley girl and so forth—must by now be an easily recognized fictional phenomenon. To the general public she is richer, better dressed (in a recognizable style), from a "better" family—usually white, Protestant and somehow "aristocratic"—and her looks are standard: Anglo-Saxon, uptilted nose, free-flowing light hair, blue eyes, and an air, an easy grace, a worldly familiarity that marks her as one who knows who she is, where she came from and where she intends to go. Her path in life is unobstructed, and she is accompanied by a universal welcome. Like Daisy Buchanan in *The Great Gatsby* her voice rings with money. Like Ellen Jaspar (Bryn Mawr) in James Michener's *Caravans* she is a "vibrant, exciting girl," but clearly "not the brain of the college . . . too good-looking for that."

And like the heroine of Ernest Hemingway's play *The Fifth Column,* another version of the universally recognized figure, she is badly educated and essentially stupid, bored while taking part in exciting and extraordinary events.

John Evans Austen, a Vassar instructor, summarized other appearances of the Vassar girl in fiction. She is the subject of stories by Grace Margaret Gallagher, herself a Vassar girl, as early as 1900. Ford Madox Ford's Vassar Girl (in *The Good Soldier*) is Florence, a woman of "nearly monstrous malice" (to quote Mark Schorer) and "yet a graduate of Vassar. I never could imagine how she did it—the queer chattery person that she was." Kathleen Millay made a minor change in the name of the place ("Matthew College"), and in a 1929 novel, *Against the Wall,* had her heroine battling the administration in order to compel it to recognize the existence of sex. Mary Finch, John Dos Passos' heroine (*USA,* 1937), becomes a class-conscious fighter for proletarian causes, and Gertrude Carrick's rebellious Flip (fine, Vassar-type pet name) in *Consider the Daisies* gets into all sorts of trouble on campus by publishing scandalous issues of the literary magazine.

The Vassar girl is, in addition, the subject of well-circulated jokes. Ruth Matthewson (Vassar '41), one of *The Group*'s admirers, quotes one: "When I saw that banner on the wall, I asked her: 'If you really went to Vassar, what are you doing in a whorehouse?' Reply: 'Just lucky, I guess.' " So when she decided to treat subject matter for which a well-established cliché existed, Mary McCarthy must have been well aware that she had inherited this heavy load of connotation. Vassar, she knew, had long been "the stock butt of musical-comedy jokes and nightclub wheezes." Everyone is aware of the scorn in the voice of the comic who uses Vassar as an adjective. "Vassar girls in general were not liked, she knew, by the world at large," Priss thinks during the wedding scene of *The Group*. "They had come to be a sort of symbol of superiority."

Clearly then, the type was there, and it was possible, if Mary McCarthy wished to do so, to use it. She knew the standing cliché, but she chose instead to create a new one, a series of individual persons, almost all of whom, because of background, education, and the period in which they live, fail to "progress." Her book takes the Vassar-Girl type—secure, well off, Protestant, by chance at the same college in the same years, by choice in the same rooming group, bright, hopeful, confident, full of contemporary theories and, most of all, sure that she was "going forth" to improve the world, a girl with a quick, retentive ear for the jargon of her time, a ready, uncritical acceptance of its cant, its theories, its advanced thinking, and a consumer's eye for what is modern and avant-garde—and submits her to the world at large for seven years. This choice was made, not of the exceptional Vassar girl with whom Mary McCarthy was determined not to be involved, but of the type *figé,* because these are the more appropriate comic figures for an essentially comic landscape on the level she wished to work, the level of social history, and the years from 1933 to 1940. The girls don't change or grow or even mature very much; they are what they were when they came to Vassar, as I have noted earlier, and they take away from Vassar attitudes that fitted without strain into the mold into which they are poured. (Or another way of putting it is to say that the ground was prepared precisely for the seeds that were allowed to mature.) Their years away from Vassar do nothing to modify them. Their pronouncements about everything could have been made as easily in Oyster Bay or Salt Lake City or in the South Tower suite in 1932. Their attitudes of wide-eyed, delighted discovery about "the world," their horror at deviations from socially acceptable norms, their sense of their years at Vassar as having been wholly idyllic, their loyalty to each other (born of social and academic class, ivied and daisied place, and similar minds), all these are constants in them, the common features for their fate which turns out to be so singly and mutually uneventful. These women, like all memorable characters in fiction, *are* immortal, unchanging, and typic. The novel, a mock chronicle, is a satire, and so the characters can be, under these circumstances, nothing else.

The novel appeared in America in November of 1963, and from the reviews it received and the word of mouth that at once went forth, the whole shape of the book, and its intention, were destined to be lost in the flood of its details: social, economic, psychiatric, sexual, medical, and domestic. It was to be talked about in these terms or in terms of its chapters, some mentioned more often than others. Everywhere the novel was given wide critical notice. Reviewers were divided, however, into two camps, both hostile. Between them was a small but loyal group of defenders. One group of detractors seemed to be unaware of Mary McCarthy as an artist of long standing with a considerable history as a novelist for whom *The Group* was a logical extension of her technique and subject matter. To these critics she was a sensationalist, writing a novel for popular consumption with some pretty heady chapters, and they wondered how such a popularity-destined novel could be worth anything. On the opposite side were critics who had followed her literary career from the beginning, who took this occasion to bemoan her passing as a serious writer, her descent into the marketplace. So blinded were they by what they regarded as a clear defection from strict, ascetic literary ranks to the fleshpots of success that they could see nothing of value or interest in the style of the novel, and in most cases they avoided or missed the point of the manner of narration. Between the two groups were a few who liked the novel well enough to consider it seriously (Norman Mailer, for example, one of the few *male* critics to treat it with considerable insight), understood it, and were brave enough to praise it publicly.

To Vassar the book came as a bombshell. First faint warning of its coming appearance was in "Class of '33 Reports" in the *Alumnae Magazine* for October. The reporter said she had read "an excerpt in *The New Yorker*" and was glad to put the class's mind at rest. "No resemblance to anyone at all." By April of 1964 the full force of alumnae dislike was felt, although the same class correspondent was still able to be a little kind to the author: "Loathed *The Group*," she said in a personal, girlish note to Mary McCarthy, "but loved your new hairdo on the Jack Paar show." For months to come, the alumnae indignation grew. One correspondent hoped "the noble image of Jacqueline Kennedy would counteract" the effect of "the keyhole peeping best-seller." Another called upon the college to "repudiate" Mary McCarthy and rescind her degree for her "catalogue of venery, a disgrace to the printed word, and a blight on the reputation of a fine institution." Only one brave correspondent from the class of '39 found the book "nerve-wracking" and "wrenching" to read, not because of its unfairness to the Vassar girl, but because she could hear "in their choral voices shattering echoes of myself and my friends." It did no good for this lone voice to point out that nowhere in the novel is Vassar attacked, or those who taught at Vassar, only the "unreachable morass" of the minds of the eight Vassar alumnae. The intramural attacks went on.

Vassar-born and -bred indignation had three years to die down (it is now reliably reported that there is a paperback copy of *The Group* in almost every dormitory room at the college) when the film of the novel appeared. Vassar need not have worried. Whether because the producers decided not to encounter the massed fury of sixty-three years of Vassar women, or because they feared institutional action (somewhat like Notre Dame's action against a film that showed it in an uncomplimentary light), whatever the cause, when the film version appeared all mention of Vassar and Poughkeepsie had been excised. The "group" of photogenic starlets became the subject of this filmed pastiche, a profusely documented story of an era. Mother Vassar was cut away; her now parentless offspring became children of the city or the times or their class.

The book made Mary McCarthy a great deal of money, made her internationally famous as only a popular novelist in our time becomes famous (in Germany alone it sold 250,000 copies), put her still-elegant profile into all sorts of unexpected places—*Vogue, Esquire,* the Jack Paar show, *Life.* She became famous, talked about, everything but critically acclaimed. Echoing her own youthful distrust, the critics took her commercial success very hard, and found all kinds of fault with the novel. They found that:

> not one of her "bleating heroines" is fated "to discover a decent, happy, conventional life." (Diana Trilling)
>
> she sets out to humiliate a group of girls "as hard to tell apart as Disney dwarfs. *The Group* celebrates everything that drags down the human spirit and boxes it in." *(New Statesman)*
>
> "in an era whose chief social phenomenon is the amalgamation of classes . . . the proliferation of details about any one group . . . does not necessarily illuminate one's understanding of it." (Louis Auchincloss)

the book is "a flatly written and incoherently structured novel that bears scarcely a trace of the wit, the sharpness and the vivacity which glowed in her earlier work." (Norman Podhoretz)

"the meaning of these characters is that they have no meaning." *(Christian Century)*

it is a "well packaged and mediocre narrative." (Maxwell Geismar)

it was "a major disappointment." (Stanley Kauffmann)

Everyone of importance reviewed it. Cyril Connelly extended his early admiration for the author of *The Oasis* to this "completely feminine pastiche . . . a privileged insight into a purely feminine world." Arthur Mizener managed the difficult feat of praising and criticizing it in one sentence: "If the characters seem grotesque to some it is because we are made to see them in unsentimental clarity, and all too human." One critic thought her "lode was petering out," and called it "tough-minded sociology." Another found that "there is no end to Mary McCarthy's cleverness, for here parody is itself parodied."

The reviewers found everything in it. Reluctant admirers were glad to discover she wasn't as good as everyone had been claiming for twenty years; old admirers, themselves getting on, were glad to be able to proclaim this a good book, at least to find good things in it.

But *The Group* had been born into a new reading world, different from the one that had received *The Groves of Academe* and *A Charmed Life,* a world already primed for the appearance of any novel that is rumored to have sexy scenes. Word *did* get around—it had been getting around ever since the publication in *Partisan Review* of one of the novel's most frank chapters, "Dottie Makes an Honest Woman of Herself." By 1964 *The Group* had sold more than one hundred thousand copies in the United States, and once the sales of paperbacks and foreign editions are known, it is probable that three quarters of a million copies will be in circulation.

The enormity of *The Group*'s success amazed its author, who had been writing the same kind of honest, direct, feminine scenes in novels like *The Company She Keeps* and *A Charmed Life* without creating any such widespread stir. Indeed, until *The Group,* no book of hers had sold more than 17,000 copies. Now she was no longer avant-garde and special, the special pet of the literati, but famous and proclaimed by a world she had never contacted directly before.

Why did the novel sell so phenomenally? For one thing it is profoundly feminine. And while this had been to some extent true of her earlier fiction it is nine times as true of *The Group:* the heroines, or leading ladies, have proliferated into nine ladies and, I have already noted, one conglomerate tenth heroine-villain, a women's college. The majority of novel-readers in this country are women, and they are as well the novel-buyers and novel-borrowers; it follows that such a book, unlike the Henry Mulcahy-inhabited *Groves of Academe* or the essaylike *Oasis* and *Cast a Cold Eye,* would intrigue a mass women's audience.

Then too, the novel has that element of gossip, "tittle-tattle" about women and women's activities which Mary McCarthy has said is the natural element of fiction. A close reading of *The Group* will provide readers of the next century with evidence of feminine concerns and preoccupations in the fourth decade of this one: "progressive" theories of breast-feeding, home economics, apartment-decorating, cooking, contraception, fashions, etc. Researchers in sociology will know what women who have passed through a major women's college by 1933 thought, their "advanced" ideas about politics and sex, their fashionably conservative ideas about class, men, parents, education. They will realize that the ideas these women professed to hold were not integral to their lives but popular abstractions, fashionable at the time. After a brief encounter with thought at college and a feeble attempt to act upon it in some way in the seven years that followed graduation, their ideas "came to nothing." Kay, the most advanced, is literally buried by the rest; even her laying-out and funeral follow a set of procedures felt by the rest to be fitting for such an occasion.

Another explanation of the success of the book lay in its liberal sprinkling of what the novel-reading public likes to call sexy scenes. Dottie's defloration, her subsequent visit to the gynecologist to provide herself with a pessary, Norine's narrative about her impotent husband, etc., satisfied the Sixties' taste for such clinical descriptions. It is possible that the documentation here outweighs the usual element of character analysis; the critic of the *Times Literary Supplement* complained that he knew "much more about Dottie's vagina than about Dottie."

The most subtle appeal to the feminine reading public, however, is the almost total absence of the author from the narrative. The reader has the fun of an eavesdropper, listening in and peeping in upon, a number of women in their pursuit of the impossible goal of happiness, without the intrusion of *the person* of the author. The voice heard in each chapter is the voice of the major character in that chapter. The accent, the clichés, the contempt for the past or for parents, the tone of probity or prevarication or girlish hope or wry humor belong to Libby, or Kay or Helena, *not* to Mary McCarthy. This ventriloquism as a narrative device is apparently so ingenious that it was missed by many critics.

It allows her to remain outside the moral questions, to avoid preaching and to do what we have always been taught is the proper approach in fiction, to teach by demonstration. Promiscuity on display becomes silent evidence of a distaste for promiscuity. The messiness of Norine's apartment and the tawdriness of Kay's are silent sermons against dirt and "modern," tasteless design. The emptiness of professed abstractions, no matter how advanced, implies a real conservatism, or at least a sense that what *was* has a higher value than what is being proposed and advocated in this frivolous way. The reader is present at the Group's dishonesty, their snobbery, their self-delusion, so that when most of their lives result in commonplaces, in contrast to their aspirations, we understand why. We have followed the process. To one critic this process of preaching by omission (or by what might be called moral visual aids), is a sign of a strong streak of puritanism in Mary McCarthy. This method at work in the moral sphere parallels her way of showing her distaste for the weakness of intellectuals by involving them in discussion and action or non-action.

The plot of *The Group* is by now, thanks to the wide circulation of the film, almost as well known as the plot of the Book of Job. The plot is a non-plot, almost a static state of being, in which the heroines *are,* continue to be, and then disappear from the scene only because the book ends (this is true of all but Kay, of course). Mary McCarthy says she had trouble making anything at all happen to her women. "They really can't develop." And they don't. Faced with the time scheme she had originally proposed—the twenty years between the inauguration of Roosevelt and the inauguration of Eisenhower—she felt she could not sustain the girls that long, especially as they all fall into the category of *figé* characters. So the time span was reduced to the years between

Kay's wedding in 1933 and her death seven years later. This was long enough, Mary McCarthy apparently felt, to make her major point, that nothing would come of them. They were destined to go nowhere.

The eight Vassar girls had occupied the South Tower suite in Main Hall in their senior year. In the Vassar system they had grouped together by choice, or rather, six of them had been together by choice and then had invited Kay and Helena, her ex-roommate, to come in with them "when they saw they could get the South Tower for themselves if they had eight in the group instead of six; it was Lakey's idea that they should invite Kay and Helena. . . ." The original six consist of Elinor Eastlake (Lakey), the madonna from Lake Forest, Chicago, "intellectual, impeccable, disdainful . . . intelligent, morbidly sensitive," rich and beautiful; Dottie Renfrew of Boston, proper and easily shocked, the oldest of the group, a devout Episcopalian, of delicate health, "eczematous complexion and a susceptible throat"; Elizabeth MacAusland (Libby) from Pittsfield, Massachusetts, pretty, an Important Personage in the college, a teller of lies, avid for success, full of slang and "with a manner of anxious conviviality"; Polly Andrews of Stockbridge, her father a victim of the Depression, a warm, charming, humanitarian human being, with a passion for original cooking, and "with an original point of view"; Priss Hartshorn of Oyster Bay, "an ashy-haired little girl who looked like a gopher," who has a slight nervous stammer, and is about to be married to a domineering young physician; and Mary Prothero (Pokey), "a fat, cheerful New York society girl with big red cheeks and yellow hair . . . very rich and lazy and good-natured."

The two outsiders are Kay Leiland Strong of Salt Lake City, bright, pretty, enthusiastic, a lover of acting, an eager student of whatever is new and modern, and a "ruthless hatred of poor people," and Helena Davison of Cleveland, who has "a puckish sense of humor," is the scholar of the group, "a short, sandy-haired girl with an appealing snub nose" and "a fondness for walking around nude that had startled the others at first. . . . In her cool character the only passion yet awakened was the passion for truth."

Actually there are nine Vassar alumnae if Norine Blake is included. Norine was a classmate, not a group-mate, a "frowsty" girl with "a tall rangy figure" who thought of herself as "political," knew who had counted at Vassar and who had not. She had envied the Group from the outside, or at least the stereotype of them, as Miss Lockwood would have called it.

This stereotype ("Poise. Social savvy. Looks. Success with men. . . . Aloof from the battle") is given to us only to reveal its falseness. Helena recognizes that "if you rolled the whole group into one girl she would be what Norine said—a rich, assured, beautiful bluestocking." She thinks that "this view of the group was so far from the facts that she could not begin to correct it." Mary McCarthy uses all the women to destroy our (and Norine's) preconceived view of the stereotype. What is left is a rubble of suffering, confused, insecure, pathetic women.

Mary McCarthy has scattered bits of autobiography into these women, in the main into Kay (as we have seen, by using her early life in New York married to Harold Johnsrud and then, later, it may be, to Edmund Wilson). Another part of her is contained in Norine's view of the stereotype. Long before, Mary McCarthy had written of the "upper" girls at Forest Ridge Convent: "The beauty and poise of the older girls were nothing like I had seen on earth. If not like angels . . . they were . . . like Olympian goddesses, tall and swift of tread." Of the Vassar upperclassmen as they appeared to her in 1929 she wrote: "The tall, dazzling girls . . . in pale sweaters and skirts, impeccable, with pearls at the throat and stately walks like goddesses." From Kay's wedding, where the group forms itself into a kind of musical-comedy opening chorus line, until the last scene where they are again gathered together in a coda, a choral ending, for Kay's funeral, the novel sets about systematically destroying Norine's (and Mary McCarthy's) view of the goddesses, reducing them to the staid, wealthy housewives of the last chapter.

Kay's marriage to Harald fails, she becomes involved in the war fever, and is then, as Mrs. Davison says, "the first American war casualty"—she falls while plane-spotting from a window in the Vassar Club. (Her death, like Martha Sinnott's at the end of *A Charmed Life,* is an accident, and it has the same ironic edge to it that Martha's had. Kay dies because she carries her passion for involvement to its extreme. She alone breaks out of the charmed, protected life of the other girls.) Norine marries the impotent, left-wing Putnam Blake, divorces him to marry a rich Jewish banker and has Ichabod, the baby she carries in a sling to Kay's funeral. Libby, herself a successful literary agent after an abortive attempt to be a literary person, marries a best-selling author of historical novels; Helena remains "single, aloof, unawakened . . . dry and distant toward the fond passion." Pokey marries a Princeton man, has three children and seems to have become richer. Polly, after an excoriating love affair, marries a young doctor and has a baby. Priss marries her pediatrician, has a baby and suffers all the agonies of his insistence on her breast-feeding it. Dottie, after a brief and violent affair, marries a wealthy mining man "who owned half the state of Arizona." Lakey escapes the fate of the "staid, settled group with husbands and children at home" by forming a lesbian alliance with a German baroness. Because of the imminence of World

War II she returns from a long stay in Italy. Like Mary McCarthy (who kept hers for so long), she is the only one to keep her "black knot at the nape of her neck" after the others have cut and permanented their hair, and like her too she has spent time at that mecca of art lovers, Settignano, the home of Bernard Berenson.

During this circular nonprogress there is ample time to document the era. Here the method Mary McCarthy adopts, the allowance to each girl of a special voice, speech characteristics and jargon, becomes part of the documentation. The Thirties rise up out of the verbal evidence: "wouldn't that have been a howl?" "a darling little dressing room," "my pride and joy," "they just about fainted," "she would die if . . . ," "Dads"—all Kay's speech; Helena's mastery of the gushing, girlish idiom of the Vassar *Alumnae Magazine;* Dottie's voice not so much punctuated with jargon (she, like Mary McCarthy, dislikes slang) as marked by an echo of her mother's speech, and sentences that start with parental reference: "Mother said. . . ." or "Mother was quite right in. . . ." Priss speaks of being "tiddly," Pokey asks "who would have thunk it?"; there is their common "such fun" and "crazy about. . . ." and Libby's veritable mine of period slang, a proliferation that indicates something about the quality of her mind. The chapter devoted to her abounds in "spiffy," "snazzy," "plu-perfect," "her latest flame," "comfy," "perish the thought," "kerplunk," etc. Critics who leaped upon the author for her use of the cliché as if it were a stylistic slip in her usually impeccable diction failed to see that the narrator's voice (Mary McCarthy's) is heard in the novel only occasionally—at the very beginning, then to introduce each girl (and even here, she told the Danish translator of *The Group,* "there is an element of mimicry . . . a take-off on the character the narrator is describing"), and then not again until the last sentence of the book. "Everything else," she says, "is in invisible quotation marks."

No alter ego for the old, constant McCarthy voice of the other novels exists in *The Group*. Once in a while she agrees with the *feelings* of a character whose voice we are hearing (twice in Helena's chapters, first as she mentally composes the Class Notes and again during her visit to Norine's apartment). We suspect that she is often agreeing with Polly, but this is not intended to be echo; the sentences, the selection of matter all are in "the normal pitch and speed and diction of one or another of the girls." The only time in direct narration that the narrator makes an appearance is to give stage directions necessary to the action of the story: "Lakey stopped the car," and so forth. These, Mary McCarthy told her Danish translator, are given in the manner of a stage manager on the scene, as in Chinese opera. In some cases, however, these directions are *themselves* part of the Voice of the character: "Libby MacAusland had a spiffy apartment in the Village." Here Libby is "seizing the ball from the narrator."

In one way or another, the novel is entirely talk, not interior, stream-of-consciousness talk, nor even internal monologue (since this is characteristic of "a kind of note-taking of sensations," but here "sensation is at a minimum") but instead what she has termed *le style indirect libre,* fairly close to direct speech, or direct writing. Helena takes notes whenever we hear her, and we know her voice through this, just as we hear Kay, in her own voice, professing her faith in brands. It is not, as some critics have remarked, that Mary McCarthy thinks she is creating character by naming the brand of coffee (Maxwell House) that Kay puts up to perk. Kay *thinks* in this way, and we are listening to her in that parenthesis—in fact she is making the parenthesis—and in the recipes that dot her scenes, recipes which, Mary McCarthy points out, are the *idées reçues* of domestic life. The long catalogue of magazines on the coffee table is not Mary McCarthy succumbing to the lure of women novelists to interior decorate (as Norman Podhoretz has claimed) but necessary to give Helena's scorn a concrete, factual shape. The recipe for Clover Club cocktails is given in Kay's voice, a tone of pride sounding in the special, "advanced," "in" information of each detail.

Now and then in the novel it is hard to assign the Voice to one girl or to two interwoven, as happens occasionally. At these times it is the Group Voice, choruses or echoes of other voices (teachers, mothers, etc.) that are being heard through theirs. The girls often serve as echoes because they are influenced by the other voices of their time, and attuned especially to the voices of the men they marry. Harald is aware of this: "But living with a woman is like living with an echo, a loud echo in Kay's case. That voice of hers got on my nerves. Meaninglessly repeating what it'd heard. Generally from me, I admit . . . I felt like some lonely captain with a parrot."

The novel's achievement is this elaborate orchestration. It is a choral work about a short period in history, to be sung mainly by feminine voices, a persuasive and illuminating song cycle. But the failure of the novel, if it fails, is that this achievement was not easily or readily recognized. It requires close reading to see the narrative method. It was recognized by so few that the method itself must be at fault. So subtle is the vocal counterpoint that most critics failed to hear it, and so they stopped listening and made facile judgments about "what Mary McCarthy is saying."

Two other elements contribute to form the intricate pattern of this social history. One is the adults in the book (here I am considering the girls, despite their ages, to be somewhat less than adults), and the other is the men. Dominant as the girls are (and the girls' college), the adults heard and seen (with the exception of Hatton, the Prothero butler, whom Mary McCarthy says is one of the mothers, and who comes to Kay's funeral in place of Mrs. Prothero and "the family") are parents, principally mothers, although an occasional father's voice is heard on the periphery.

As the book was first planned, this mother-daughter relationship was to be a large part of the story, as significant for it as it is, for example, for "Appalachian Revolution," where the married women act always by consultation with their mothers. In the *Paris Review* (1961) Mary McCarthy said of *The Group:* "All their mothers are in it. The fathers vaguely figure off stage . . . but the mothers are really monumentally present." By the time the novel appeared the mothers had sunk in importance. Not one of them is monumental. They have become merely a dimension, a level, a small part of the story that contributes some richness to it. Lakey's mother does not appear (Helena claims Lakey is *sui generis*); Kay's mother arrives neither for her wedding (the Group Voice notes the "absence of parents or *any* older person") nor for her funeral; Pokey's mother is congealed in money, allowing Hatton to take her place; Helena's mother is merely a spectator or, at most, an occasional commentator; Priss' is a vague echo, "an advanced society woman" and nothing more. Only Mrs. Renfrew, Dottie's mother, has a role, a Voice, and perhaps she is intended to represent all the rest, the figure of the Mother. She comes to the foreground of the group view after they have said that they were

> not afraid of being radical either; they could see the good Roosevelt was doing, despite what Mother and Dad said . . . the worst fate, they utterly agreed, would be to become like Mother and Dad, stuffy and frightened. Not one of them, if

> she could help it, was going to marry a banker or a cold-fish corporation lawyer, like so many of Mother's generation.

Dottie begins to echo her mother as soon as she meets Dick Brown at the wedding:

> She and Mother had talked it over and agreed that if you were in love and engaged to a nice young man you perhaps ought to have relations once to make sure of a happy adjustment. Mother, who was very youthful and modern, knew of some very sad cases within her own circle of friends where the man and the woman just didn't fit down there and ought never to have been married.

When she goes back to his room, and while she is losing her virginity, she feels "stuffed with interesting thoughts that she could only confide in Mother," certainly not in Dick beside whom she is lying. At one point she wonders what the Group and Mother might be thinking, and after the Event takes place she finds herself evaluating the experience by referring to Mother's instructions in the matter. With Dick sleeping beside her, "Dottie's thoughts flew affectionately to Mother, class of 1908." Mrs. Renfrew, "a great believer in love," later hears the story of this night and gravely questions her daughter about the physical aspects of the affair. She is entirely understanding and, for all her limitations (as Mary McCarthy explained to the translator), she "exemplifies the varieties of the old American upper middle-class conscience, civic responsibility, alert feeling." Dottie's (and Mary McCarthy's) admiration for Mrs. Renfrew is consistent with the younger Mary's thinking about "the older generation," of which the Vassar *emeritae,* Miss Mackay, called Miss Gowrie, and Miss Atkinson, are all real-life representatives. After Dottie's confession to her mother in Boston, the irony of the relationship becomes clear to Mrs. Renfrew:

> [She] was aware of the oddity of this situation, in which the roles were reversed, and the daughter was hurrying herself into a "suitable" marriage while the mother was pleading with her to seek out an unsuitable rake. This was, apparently, that "gulf between the generations" that had been discussed at her class reunion last June; one of the faculty members of Mrs. Renfrew's class had stated it as a generalization that this new crop of girls was far less idealistic, less disinterested, as a body of educated women, than their mothers had been.

But Dottie ignored her mother's old-fashioned advice "to be true to your own lights in this. If you love Dick . . ." and marries the wealthy Arizonan, refusing to abandon her inherited class values even though her mother gives her permission to do so. At this point Dottie disappears from the novel except to wait briefly on the dock for Lakey's arrival from Italy. She is represented at the funeral, of course, by her mother.

Originally, I suspect, all the girls were destined, after a generation, to appear more conservative, more rigid, more foolish and less morally courageous and more complacent than the mothers they had been determined not to resemble in the first pages of the book. But it was apparently less interesting, perhaps too complex, to juggle two generations of Voices at once, so Mary McCarthy compromised with one set which, on occasion, will echo the other. Dottie and her mother are the major remaining evidence of a relationship and a level of meaning once intended to be important.

The second element of the novel contributing to its dense texture is the male characters. As they often are in Mary McCarthy's fiction, they are nasty, demonic, weak, and, in one way or another, somewhat unpleasant. Louis Auchincloss writes: "The real rocks on which the crafts of the Vassar girls founder are not the confusions of twentieth century progress but the cruelties of twentieth century men . . . one must turn back to the novels of Ellen Glasgow for a greater collection of cads than that which lies in wait for Vassar '33." Mary McCarthy admits that "ninety percent of the men in the book are awful." One (Gus) is a nonentity, one (Dick) an "unhappy individual, an impossible person for Dottie to have an affair with," and "Mr. Davison is okay," but the others are "so terrible." "Those Vassar girls," she told an interviewer, "did not marry well."

Mary McCarthy's male characters have in general been unsubstantial fellows like John Sinnott; Polly's husband, Dr. Ridgeley; Priss' husband—unless they were malevolent like Miles Murphy, Henry Mulcahy, Harald Petersen, or "spoiled" figures like Jim Barnett. Accosted by this fact she says that in real life she prefers men to women but that in her writing her sympathetic men "tend to be rather shadowy." Love does not fail in her novels, only the male lovers. The substantial, completely realized male characters are the monsters; the few good ones, as she says, are flat and shadowy. So it becomes possible, after *The Group,* to generalize by saying that it is women who *interest* Mary McCarthy (the main woman, at first, being herself) because she knows and understands them, or at least makes fortunate guesses about what makes them the way they are. Men, whom she says she likes, she knows less about (as is no doubt inevitable to a woman writer) and rarely sees them as heroic or thoroughly decent or even likable. They all suffer from the *grand mal* of being male, and their wives, or mistresses or women friends suffer, nobly rise above them or, like a body dealing with a transplant of foreign tissue, reject them utterly and irrevocably. The women are morally superior to their men (Harald claims Kay killed herself to prove this to him, and Martha Sinnott's moral posture is better than her doctor's to whom she goes for advice), far more sensitive and capable of insights into their situation. In Ernest Hemingway the landscapes are customarily full of men without women; in Mary McCarthy almost the opposite is true.

Despite *The Group*'s great popular appeal, and its success as an experiment in fictional Voice, it is, to my mind, a lesser work than *The Groves of Academe* or even *The Oasis* and *The Company She Keeps.* Its wit is more diffuse, the writing less pointed and more haphazard, so that it seems to be making its points indirectly, by omission. It is more shapeless than the other books (the inclusion of the Prothero-Hatten chapter pushes it out of shape in one direction, and there are other tangents like it), and so it seems at times to be "out of control," to fall away into the very welter of detail that is part of its method. The mass of detail obscures other necessary facts too: for example, that it is only on Libby's prevaricating word and Harald's embittered ones that Kay is said to be a suicide. There is so much talk in that chapter, so much documentation, that the reader is likely to forget Libby's propensity and Harald's character and remember only the echo of their remarks. This happened, of course, to many critics who got lost in the Voices, or did not remember the nature of the Voice giving information.

The Group is a negative book, a novel that brings bad "news," that conveys a hopeless, retrograde message. This is, of course, true of *The Oasis,* but for some reason it is more oppressive in *The Group* because *the number* of examples of hopelessness abound. And it is unselective, or seems to be so because of the wealth of detail. Everything that could be remembered of that time and that place has been put in so that the essential outline, often the essential point, is obscured. To my mind, the virtues of the novel, many as they are, do not outweigh its drawbacks. Artistically interesting and fine in many places, it does not stand in the front rank of the fiction of Mary McCarthy.

A final note: despite the denials of all Vassar women that these girls do not exist, and the Class of 1933 that they were not in *their* class, the eight heroines are all based on real persons, at least in part, and four are easily and readily identifiable by their classmates (if they wished to make the effort). Some changes have been made in them, some characteristics played down and others substituted, but as usual Mary McCarthy has not moved very far from the Fact, the core of truth. It is for this reason, no doubt, that the denials have been so fierce and so constant.

* * *

Mary McCarthy now lives in Paris with James West, in a cooperative apartment on the rue de Rennes which they bought toward the beginning of their marriage. She is a slender, graying and unusually attractive woman who looks younger than her fifty-five years. In her sixth year of residence in France she is highly vocal about her dislike of Paris and Parisians. She dislikes French intellectuals, especially writers like Jean-Paul Sartre and Simone de Beauvoir, whom she accuses of being "arid, lacking a sense of humor, or humility. Her memoirs are a parody of the female intellectual. She is terribly solemn, pompous and unoriginal. I hate her." Her dislike of Simone de Beauvoir is profound and complex. When questioned about her, she says: "She's an enemy," and then proceeds to describe her essentially "bourgeoise" mind, her insensitivity, her blindness to everything not French.

Mary McCarthy has failed to find a community, an intellectual Group, among French writers. She finds them cold, self-involved and uninterested in anyone but themselves. Her friends in Paris are mostly not French, and it is for this reason that she admits she would rather live in Rome or Warsaw. She says that, if it becomes possible, she would like to return to America. To a recent interviewer she said, "I work better there. If a writer doesn't hear his own language, his writing feels it." From all evidence she is happy with her fourth husband, "not," as Katharine Whitehorn wrote in the London *Observer,* "at last, but once more."

She is at work now on her sixth novel, a trial chapter of which, entitled *Birds of America,* appeared last year in *Southern Review.* The chapter has since been discarded, but the theme and two main characters remain. It is, apparently, a *bildungsroman,* an apprenticeship novel, in which a young man, Peter Levi, child of divorced parents and son of a sensitive, talented and beloved mother with whom he now lives, grows to maturity, putting his childhood behind him. In outline and character the story seems to be heavily autobiographical. Peter, a Candide figure, is related to Reuel, and Rosamund Brown to Reuel's mother. The Voice heard in the chapter is Peter's, first his own directly (there may be a chapter of his aphorisms, called Peter's Laws, that will summarize his wisdom on the subject of adults) and then the echo of his mother's Voice heard through his. The title reflects Peter's passion for birds, in a wildlife sanctuary on Cape Cod, rather than human beings; his mother, for whom he once in his early teens, had a deep and passionate love, is the one exception.

At the same time Mary McCarthy has recently written a long critical study of Ivy Compton-Burnett, whom she very much admires, and is thinking of doing a "tall, thin book," a study of Gothic architecture in Western Europe. She has been spending her free weekends traveling about her area of France looking at notable examples of the period.

What of the others in her history? Her son, Reuel Wilson,

is twenty-nine, married to a painter; he is now somewhat aloof from both his parents. He is a candidate for his Ph.D. in Slavic languages, in which he has his M.A. The two younger McCarthy brothers, Sheridan and Preston, have lived obscure lives in contrast with their well-known brother and sister. Sheridan was "in" insurance in Chicago and was the only one of the four children to remain a Catholic; married to a girl from Minneapolis, he had two children and died in October 1966. Preston (whose given name his sister used for a character in *The Oasis*) married a Scarsdale, New York, girl, works in a bank, and now lives with his wife and children on the East Coast. Her brother Kevin is well known as an actor on the screen, television, and the legitimate stage; Kevin and Mary still bear a close physical resemblance to each other.

In the fifth decade of her life, Mary McCarthy is unique among American writers for her versatility. She is a novelist whose novels are often tracts displaying her disappointment that people are not what they profess to be (like the inhabitants of New Leeds where "everybody was 'artistic' and nobody was an artist"), especially intellectuals in and out of the universities, that persons with intelligence are not also men of goodwill. She is a noted autobiographer whose autobiographical work is riddled with fiction, and a fiction writer who leans heavily, sometimes embarrassingly, upon autobiography. She is an aesthetician in fiction, art, and architecture, a critic of both the theatre and the literature of her time. Her uniqueness lies partly in her readiness to do battle, her willingness to attack in every direction, without concern for the barriers of established reputation.

At one time or another, in speech or in writing, she has assailed such literary holies as J. D. Salinger (*Franny and Zooey* "suffers from this terrible sort of metropolitan sentimentality, and it's so narcissistic, so false, so calculated, combining the plain man with an absolutely megalomaniac egoism"), critic Kenneth Tynan ("His wit and humor... have the middle-aged quality of long-suffering—the classic, henpecked humor of the drama reviewer wedded to a seat on the aisle"), playwright Tennessee Williams, scholar-writer Leon Edel ("Those Henry James books are abysmal. This is one of those open secrets that everybody thinks and nobody says. Every time a new book in this long, biographical series comes out you wait.... You look around and nobody else says anything, not a soul"). She has expressed a dislike of the works of Graham Greene ("Religion hinted at in this manner becomes a form of obscenity"), Ernest Hemingway, Virginia Woolf, Katherine Mansfield, most American playwrights, and most English playwrights *except* John Osborne's in his first play. And *this* seeming softening was later corrected when she reviewed Osborne's fifth play by saying she was still waiting for his second.

She can also turn her fire on somewhat more intangible notions: ambition unaccompanied by talent; success that is popular, widespread, and commercial; Europeans, who are the greatest materialists; Parisians, who are "insular, parochial and utterly uninterested in foreigners"; Americans in the 1960's, who have "deteriorated terribly... those weak, adenoidal, odious men and their slack-bodied slovenly women." She has adamantly maintained her strong political views in which she continues to admire the dissident (Trotsky, especially), and to profess her libertarian socialism, her religious views ("I don't believe in God... I prefer to be called an atheist, although I realize it is a more difficult position to defend than being an agnostic"), and her views on women writers, most of whom she dislikes, especially "that whole sensibility school. I am for the ones who represent sense, and so was Jane Austen."

Her enthusiasms are less publicized but equally passionate. Sometimes they light in unlikely and unpredictable places, on Joseph Heller's *Catch 22,* for example, or on William Burroughs' *Naked Lunch.* More predictable is her passionate admiration for Tolstoy, Flaubert, George Eliot, Dickens, and "all the Elizabethans." She very much likes the work of Robert Lowell (a close friend), John Dos Passos (whose *USA* she thinks is underestimated now), the *Studs Lonigan* books of James Farrell, William Faulkner, much of the work of Saul Bellow, the stories of V. S. Pritchett, F. Scott Fitzgerald's *The Great Gatsby* and some of his stories, some of the work of Alberto Moravia. She admires the novels of Natalie Sarraute (a personal friend, but she sees no reason why friendship should stand in the way of admiring a friend's work), and is a great and vocal enthusiast for Nabokov's *Pale Fire.* Among women writers she approves of Jane Austen, Isak Dinesen, Eudora Welty, the late scholar and philosopher Simone Weil (whose essay on the *Iliad* she translated into English), her close friend Hannah Arendt (she reviewed *The Human Condition* almost ecstatically, praising her "combination of tremendous intellectual power with great common sense") and the young novelist, Alison Lurie, who is often compared to Mary McCarthy. One well-established writer she believes is due for a stern reexamination: Henry James. And she would like to see a reassessment done of Émile Zola.

Her wit is her major weapon and, like Martha Sinnott, she knows "that this rather scares people." She is direct to the point of wounding and committed to absolute honesty, possessed of an irresistible urge to tell the truth, like Martha who "only spoke the literal truth—that was her peculiarity." She remains suspicious of motives, even her own, and, as

Lionel Trilling has phrased it in another context, always asks of herself and others "what might lie behind our good impulses." She is still angry enough about a number of things to be a successful satirist, and she remains that unusual variety of American writer, one blessedly encumbered with intellect.

She is a conscious stylist of the first rank. To resort again to Lionel Trilling, this time to his comment that Scott Fitzgerald's greatness is to be seen "where eventually all a writer's qualities have their truest existence—in his style," it is clear that in Mary McCarthy's case too her sentences, the way they are pitched, their elegant form and variety, are instrumental in defining the tone of her fiction. Her early tendency was to be epigrammatic, to use imagery (especially religious imagery) heavily, to stud her prose with foreign words and phrases, to resort often to the balance and antithesis of classical style, and to use frequent classical allusion. Some of this has passed. She has an affection for highly allusive talk, a fondness for generalization, a partiality for parody of the verbiage and the Voices of her time. She herself cannot write badly; she has a horror of anyone, no matter how famous, who does.

She seems to me to bear the marks, in her writing of fiction, of a displaced person, the "stranger to this ground," orphaned, excluded, the Westerner come East, the Catholic among Protestants, the end girl of the rooming group, the American abroad. Despite this, she makes very little effort to gain acceptance except on her own strict terms; in fact, it may be that the cutting edge of her wit and her fine style have been sharpened by her "outside" experiences.

She is pessimistic about the occupants of the inner circle. She seems to share Cyril Connolly's pessimism, which he expressed upon resigning his editorship of *Horizon:* "It is closing time in the gardens of the West, and from now on an artist will be judged only by the resonance of his solitude or the quality of his despair." Her despair at the tragic velocity of lives led without progress, at the dishonesty of the intellectuals, at the pretenses of Art, her contempt for cant, have not diminished with time. She has aged and matured, but not softened. Katherine Anne Porter has called her "in some ways the worst-tempered woman in American letters." She is the landwrecker McCarthy, like Lord Byron brilliant and from her targets' point of view, unsound.

She once stated her intention to abandon her lifelong fictional search for her identity, for self, although the search had not led to any conclusive discoveries. She seems to have settled for Bossuet's dictum: "We must know ourselves to the pitch of being horrified." She has expressed her horror, over and over, and then moved on to more objective Voices. She wants badly now to lose permanently her own dominating Voice.

She remains entirely frank in her views, with no hint of diplomacy or tact, forthright about her likes and dislikes. She retains her fondness for shock as a method, from her earliest days when she "lost her faith" at the convent retreat until the moment at a recent Vassar alumnae tea in Washington, D.C., when she announced blithely that if she had a daughter she would send her to Radcliffe. This may be viewed as a persistent childishness; it is also, it seems, a native iconoclasm, a habit of mind, that is natural and instinctive to her, the reformer who is willing to discard the baby in order to be permanently rid of the bath water."

She shares Emily Dickinson's admission to Colonel Higginson that "candor is the only wile," and she has built a career, as someone has said, on candor and dissent. She has always regarded sex as comic or grotesque, and professes a lack of interest in "happy" sex in fiction. She is unforgiving to her enemies and is no more charitable toward human stupidity than she is to bad writing. She is a David against the social, economic, intellectual and cultural Goliaths of the twentieth century, and she relishes the role.

She has never lost her faith in the Fact and her reliance upon it in her novels. Her fiction is really dramatized theses, orations with figures. Her special purview has been the facts of feminine existence that other writers, especially other women, have shied away from as indelicate. As Maxwell Geismar said of Saul Bellow, she is a novelist in spite of herself, for all her instincts are toward the informal essay raised to the level of fiction. Dwight Macdonald has called her fiction "a series of reviews of people's performances" rather than a direct vision of the performances themselves. In the process of the review we learn her standards and hear her rather stern, sometimes almost puritanical moral judgments. Her criticism, like her fiction, is uncorrupted by compassion, and she writes it with a sense of mission, of vocation. She is an advocate of common sense, the concrete, the real, and the authentic.

She is a writer upon whom nothing has been lost. Her memory is so faultless that the documentation of *The Group* was done without any recourse to research. She says that only after the book was finished did she discover that she had in her file an alumnae report of the Class of '33. She is economical and uses a great deal of what she remembers. If a novel is an attempt to preserve the moment that passes, she is constantly searching her memory for evidences of that moment, combing her experience for its facts. Her tendency in fiction is to document, to catalogue, to shore up with detail. Like an attorney cross-examining a witness, she says to her fictional characters, taken from the world she knows and from her own life, "I want only the *facts.*"

Finally, she is aware of the perils of intellect at the same time that she herself relies heavily upon it. Her subject matter is feminine, but she approaches it by means of a thoroughly masculine mind. She distrusts all orthodoxies and authorities while maintaining the most severe orthodoxy of them all, a stern, conservative, personal sense of individual freedom in every area of contemporary life.

Mary McCarthy
Paris '62
Rivers

Portrait of Mary McCarthy by Larry R
Courtesy of Mr. and Mrs. Stanley S. A